SpringerBriefs in Law

More information about this series at http://www.springer.com/series/10164

Christoph Kleineberg

Vertical Integration and Regulation

An Analysis of Vertical Unbundling from a Competition Law and Competition Economics Perspective

Springer

Christoph Kleineberg
Competition & Regulation Institute
Leuphana University of Lüneburg
Lüneburg, Germany

ISSN 2192-855X ISSN 2192-8568 (electronic)
SpringerBriefs in Law
ISBN 978-3-030-11357-5 ISBN 978-3-030-11358-2 (eBook)
https://doi.org/10.1007/978-3-030-11358-2

Library of Congress Control Number: 2018967414

This Springer imprint is published by the registered company Springer Nature Switzerland AG
The registered company address is: Gewerbestrasse 11, 6330 Cham, Switzerland

Acknowledgements

I would like to express my gratitude for a number of people who have supported me in the writing process of this book. First and foremost, I want to thank my wife Annika Melles who has supported me throughout the writing process, made helpful remarks, motivated me to finish the work and proofread all drafts.

In addition, I would like to thank my supervisors Prof. Dr. Jörg Philipp Terhechte and Prof. Dr. Thomas Wein for the good and fruitful supervision and the comprehensive advice I received.

Finally, I would like to thank Callee Anne Davis for the support by proofreading several drafts.

Contents

Abbreviations

AC	Average costs
CPR	Cost-Price-Regulation
D	Demand
ECHR	European Convention of Human Rights
ECJ	European Court of Justice
EU	European Union
GATT	General Agreement on Tariffs and Trade
GG	Grundgesetz (in English: "German Basic Law")
GWB	Gesetz gegen Wettbewerbsbeschränkungen (in English: "German Act against Restraints of Competition")
MC	Marginal costs
MR	Marginal revenue
MTS	Markttransparenzstelle (in English: "Market Transparency Unit")
Ofcom	Office of Communications
Ofgem	Office of Gas and Electricity Markets
Ofwat	Economic Regulator of Water Sector in England and Wales
ORR	Office of Rail and Road
RPM	Resale price maintenance
TEU	Treaty on the European Union in the version of Lisbon (frequently referred to as part of the "Lisbon Treaty")
TFEU	Treaty on the functioning of the European Union (frequently referred to as part of the "Lisbon Treaty")
UK	United Kingdom
USA	United States of America
WTO	World Trade Organisation

List of Figures

Chapter 1
Introduction

Markets have been widely discussed and examined by the general public, politicians, economists, lawyers and regulators as well as competition authorities in many countries. Given the direct effect of well- or malfunctioning markets on consumers' expenses, there is a broad debate about which measures should be implemented. Politicians, in particular, strongly favour increasing the competitiveness of markets, because they hope that in doing so this would lead to lower product or service prices which result in increased approval by the electorate.

Comprehensive examination and broad interest on the issue has resulted in numerous proposals on how to stimulate competition in markets, lower prices, increase consumer welfare and maximize economic welfare as a whole.[1]

Nevertheless, one of the strongest tools with the widest-reaching consequences in the field of regulation, namely the idea of unbundling, has not yet been mentioned in these debates. It has been called the "ultima ratio" of regulation law.[2] Due to its controversial character and the significant interference of unbundling with fundamental freedoms such as the freedom of property and occupational freedom, unbundling has not been included as a tool of regulation by the German Act against Restraints of Competition or the Treaty on the European Union (TEU) and the Treaty on the Functioning of the European Union (TFEU) on the European Union (EU) level.[3]

In the first section of this thesis, the subject of investigation (Sect. 1.1) and the aim of investigation (Sect. 1.2) are presented. Thereafter, objections to research in this particular field are presented and various responses are provided (Sect. 1.3). Finally, the course of investigation (Sect. 1.4) is outlined.

---

[1]See Conrad (2017), pp. 19–55; Fritsch (2010), pp. 21 ff.; Blundell et al. (1999), pp. 529–554; Zhang et al. (2008), pp. 159–178; critically to this approach Conover and Miller (2010); Lado et al. (1997), pp. 110–141.

[2]See Green Party in the Federal German Parlament (2017).

[3]For the significance of competition in and through the European Union see Terhechte (2004), pp. 107–126.

C. Kleineberg, *Vertical Integration and Regulation*, SpringerBriefs in Law,
https://doi.org/10.1007/978-3-030-11358-2_1

1.1 Subject of Investigation

The subject of study in a broader sense is how to increase competition in markets in general. In a very narrow sense, the subject of study is an assessment of the effects unbundling would have on a particular market or how vertical integration might already affect competition in markets.

In conclusion, the research questions are: Which effect does vertical integration may have in market sectors with particular characteristics? Which regulatory measures could be applied in order to enable or stimulate competition?

Early scientific work and especially early rulings of Courts in the USA connected vertical integration closely with the establishment of monopolies.[4] Since there is no scientific consensus on the effect of vertical integration, an assessment of actual and possible effects of vertical integration has to consider a number of environmental factors as well as market characteristics. Therefore, it is impossible to come up with simple solutions. The idea of this thesis is to rather determine factors that are crucial for vertical integration and assess their effect. In order to answer the question of whether or not vertical integration has a positive or negative effect for markets, competition on markets and consequently consumer and total welfare, a case by case assessment has to be conducted. The German Federal Cartel Office is repeatedly investigating individual markets.[5] This investigation has been enabled after the amendment of the German Act against Restraints of Competition (GWB) and the introduction of §32 GWB. However, no investigation has been conducted to assess and quantify the potential harm to competition based on the level of vertical integration of a market.

1.2 Aim of the Investigation

This investigation aims to assess the impact vertical integration has on markets with particular characteristics. The investigation analyses whether unbundling in a market is likely to increase competition or not. Furthermore, the application of additional means that have not yet been considered by the European and German competition authorities as well as the European and German regulation authorities is assessed.

---

[4]See Adelman (1949), pp. 27–77; Edwards (1953), pp. 404–410; Comanor (1967), pp. 254–265; Adelman (1955), pp. 281–330; Canes (1976), pp. 103–120.

[5]Since 2005 the Federal German Cartel Office has investigated several sectors, namely the cement industry, the submetering industry, the market power in the grocery industry, the dual waste management system, the rolled asphalt industry, the district heating industry, the natural gas industry, the milk industry, the gasoline industry, the energy production and sales industry, the heating current sector and the outdoor advertising sector. For individual reports see Federal German Cartel Office (2017).

The underlying aim of the investigation conducted in this work is to identify legal amendments or regulatory tools, which upon application increase competition. In order to do so, a model which evaluates the effect of vertical integration is applied to the regulatory framework and its limitations given current German Basic Law and European Treaties.[6] The assessment will propose various amendments on how to increase competition and as a result, increase consumer welfare and societal welfare on vertically integrated markets. Legal amendments are suggested if the application of a competition or regulatory tool, which is prohibited by constitutional or EU law is expected to have a positive effect.

1.3 Objections to the Investigation

Economists in particular, are raising objections to research on the effects of vertical integration on markets by simply citing the elimination of double marginalisation as its core character.[7]

This assumption is based on the perfectly competitive market in the downstream level. If there were perfect competition on the downstream level and a monopoly or oligopoly profit on the upstream level, why should an enterprise engage in downstream operations at all? According to that logic, it would be most profitable to engage in upstream operations and not have any capital bound in operations that would not generate additional profit.

In contrast, it is more likely that vertically integrated enterprises have a significant interest in protecting their own downstream operations where they generate additional profits or at least cover their costs. If they do not enjoy economics of scale or if they even have diseconomies of scale, they would have an incentive to harm competing firms, especially fringe firms. As a result, it is necessary to investigate what (positive as well as negative) effects vertical integration has and whether or not measures to protect or facilitate competition need to be implemented.

1.4 Course of Investigation

An assessment of the effects of vertical integration on markets requires a definition of the core terms of regulation and a presentation of the regulatory tools that are already in existence in markets (Sect. 2.1). Additionally, it is necessary to be aware of scholarly literature which considers the topic of vertical integration. Because the

---

[6]For the interdependencies of basic rights and (regulation) law see Hatje and Nettesheim (2008); Jarass (2006), pp. 1089–1094.

[7]See Knieps (2008), chapter 7; Haucap et al. (2008), pp. 27–65; Gaudet and Van Long (1996), pp. 409–432.

issue of vertical integration is addressed in the academic fields of economics and law, scientific literature from the economic (Sect. 2.2) and legal (Sect. 2.3) field are summarised and presented.

In order to conduct a proper scientific investigation, a scientific model to evaluate the effect of vertical integration is presented (Chap. 3). It serves as a theoretical and legal background, as well as an economic justification for the assessment of the impact of vertical integration. An assessment of the impact of vertical integration allows for various conclusions on the necessity of unbundling tools to be drawn at a later stage.

Consequently, theses about the protection of competition in markets or industrial sectors with particular characteristics are presented (Chap. 4). These theses are elaborated by outlining the current legal obligations enterprises already have with regard to this particular aspect. Afterwards the (legal and economic) shortcomings are presented and the constitutional framework for amendments is presented. The last step in order to justify the theses is the presentation of suggested legal amendments.

Finally, a conclusion of the effect of vertical integration on markets and competition, as well as recommended measures to stimulate competition is drawn (Chap. 5).

References

Adelman MA (1949) Integration and antitrust policy. Harvard Law Rev 63(1):27–77

Adelman MA (1955) Concept and statistical measures of vertical integration. In: Business concentration and price policy, pp 281–330

Blundell R, Griffith R, Van Reenen J (1999) Market share, market value and innovation in a panel of british manufacturing firms. Rev Econ Stud 66(3):529–554

Canes ME (1976) The vertical integration of oil firms. In: Allingham B (ed) Resource allocation and economic policy. Palgrave Macmillan, London, pp 103–120

Comanor WS (1967) Vertical mergers, market powers, and the antitrust laws. Am Econ Rev 57 (2):254–265

Conover CJ, Miller TP (2010) Why a public plan is unnecessary to stimulate competition. American Enterprise Institute for Public Policy Research, Working papers No. 162

Conrad CA (2017) Wirtschaftspolitik: Eine praxisorientierte Einführung. Springer Gabler. Wiesbaden. Kapitel Markt und Wettbewerb. pp 19–55

Edwards CD (1953) Vertical integration and the monopoly problem. J Mark 17(4):404–410

Federal German Cartel Office (2017) Sektoruntersuchungen, online. http://www.bundeskartellamt.de/DE/Wirtschaftsbereiche/Sektoruntersuchungen/sektoruntersuchungen_node.html. Last accessed 2018-11-22, 09:30 hours

Fritsch M (2010) Marktversagen und Wirtschaftspolitik: Mikroökonomische Grundlagen staatlichen Handelns, 8th edn. Verlag Franz Vahlen, Munich

Gaudet G, Van Long N (1996) Vertical integration, foreclosure, and profits in the presence of double marginalization. J Econ Manage Strategy 5(3):409–432

Green Party in the Federal German Parliament (2017) Entschließungsantrag der Fraktion Bündnis 90/Die Grünen im Bundestag zu der dritten Beratung des Gesetzentwurfs der Bundesregierung, Bundestag-Drucksache 18/11456, vom 08.03.2017

Hatje A, Nettesheim M (eds) Grundrechtsschutz im Dreieck von nationalem, europäischem und internationalem Recht. Europarecht. Beiheft 1/2008

Haucap J, Heimeshoff U, Uhde A (2008) Vertikale Entflechtung netzgebundener Industrien: Kosten und Nutzen aus ökonomischer Sicht. In: Gesellschaft für öffentliche Wirtschaft (ed) Auswirkungen der Globalisierung auf die öffentlichen Banken: Trennung von Infrastruktur und Betrieb, Beiträge zur öffentlichen Wirtschaft 26, Berlin, pp 27–65

Jarass HD (2006) Der grundrechtliche Eigentumsschutz im EU-Recht. Neue Zeitschrift für Verwaltungsrecht: 1089-1094

Knieps G (2008) Wettbewerbsökonomie: Regulierungstheorie, Industrieökonomie, Wettbe werbspolitik. Chapter 7 Vertikale Bindungen. Springer, Heidelberg

Lado AA, Boyd NG, Hanlon SC (1997) Competition, cooperation, and the search for economic rents. A syncretic model. Acad Manage Rev 22(1):110–141

Terhechte JP (2004) Die Rolle des Wettbewerbsrechts in der europäischen Verfassung. In: Hatje T (ed) Das Binnenmarktziel in der Europäischen Verfassung. Europarecht. Beiheft 3/2004, pp 107–126

Zhang Y-F, Parker D, Kirkpatrick C (2008) Electricity sector reform in developing countries: an econometric assessment of the effects of privatization, competition and regulation. J Regul Econ 33(2):159–178

Chapter 2
Theoretical Discussion of Vertical Integration and Regulation

The core focus of this thesis is to assess the degree of regulation required to ensure the highest level of societal welfare, the lowest (consumer) prices and the most competition on markets. To properly conduct the assessment, all terms need to be defined. As a first step, the general concept of regulation is presented (Sect. 2.1). Afterwards the legal aspects of vertical integration (Sect. 2.2) and the economic aspects of vertical integration (Sect. 2.3) are outlined in order to properly situate the investigation in the body of the existing literature.

The issue of vertical integration needs to be evaluated from a legal, as well as from an economic perspective. The phrase vertical integration refers to the business structure of an enterprise.[1]

2.1 General Concept of Regulation

In order to present the concept of regulation, the general idea of regulation, its underlying aims, its organisation and its core functions will be discussed. In comparison to competition law, regulation law has appeared in the public eye after-market failure was constituted. When exploring the origin and meaning of the term "regulation", an assessment of the exact wording of the term is the first obvious criterion to start the investigation. The term "regulation" or "to regulate" is usually used in legal or economic matters. The Oxford Dictionary of English defines the verb "regulate" as "to control something especially a business activity by means of rules and regulation".[2] Based on this definition, which can also be

[1]Edwards (1953), pp. 404.
[2]Hornby and Turnbull (2010).

C. Kleineberg, *Vertical Integration and Regulation*, SpringerBriefs in Law,
https://doi.org/10.1007/978-3-030-11358-2_2

found in other dictionaries, the word regulation refers to the body of legal norms that are affecting every (possible) action of single businesses or of industries as a whole. Still a legal definition of the term "regulation" remains missing.[3]

The concepts of regulation are presented for regulation law in general (Sect. 2.1.1), the general regulation of economics (Sect. 2.1.2) as well as sector specific regulation in case of particular markets (Sect. 2.1.3). Because the suggested amendments have to be in accordance with German constitutional law, European law and international law, the final sub-section presents the boundaries stemming from constitutional law and fundamental rights of the German Basic Law and the Treaties of the European Union (Sect. 2.1.4).

2.1.1 General Regulation Law

The term "regulation" can be applied very broadly to all measures which directly or indirectly and possibly or actually have an effect on any actions of market participants. The legal term of regulation has a narrower scope and refers to the body of legal norms that aim to protect competition by defining framework conditions. Nevertheless, it is difficult to distinguish competition from regulation law. Both strive to protect competition, although competition law focuses more on market conduct of individual participants rather than structural aspects. Still, some measures like market access or net access can be considered part of competition and regulation law.[4]

With regard to economic theory, regulation is a necessary means to compensating for the existence of imperfect markets. Economists base their original models on the idea of a perfectly competitive market. Perfectly competitive markets have the following assumptions[5]:

- There are no preferences (no personal preferences, time preferences, preferences of a single kind or geographical preferences).
- The entire market is fully transparent.
- There is full homogeneity among all goods.
- All market participants immediately react to changes of single market variables.
- Every market participant wants to maximise his/her utility.

Because few (if any) markets possess these characteristics, particular means are required to make up for the shortcomings of a market. Still, these means are not supposed to limit competition and competitive behaviour of market participants.

[3]There is no legal consensus on whether or not regulation law refers to a particular source and field of law, see Basedow (2004), pp. 3–20; Voßkuhle (2003), pp. 266–335; Eifert (2006), § 19.

[4]See Kühling (2004).

[5]See Robinson (1934), pp. 104–120; Stigler (1957), pp. 1–17; Aumann (1964), pp. 39–50; Anderson (1992), Chap. 14.

They rather protect the market from anti-competitive market behaviour of participants that is enabled by the existence of the imperfect market or in other words by the lack of particular characteristics of the perfect market.[6]

2.1.2 General Regulation Economics

The general economic approach is embodied in the necessity to stimulate and protect competition. Competition is the tool to creating the highest aggregation of goods and services. By competing over scarce resources, the interactions in a market are assumed to be a stimulus for efficiency and continuous improvements. If markets fail to provide an efficient market result, regulation is expected to fix this shortcoming and eventually lead to an efficient (or optimal[7]) market result.

According to Hayek (1969), competition can be perceived as an investigative process over the course of which equilibrium is determined. This forms the foundation of Adam Smith's ideology which allows the invisible hand to find the optimal place. Still, in some circumstances markets fail and do not provide a sufficient market result on their own.[8]

Reasons for market failure can be external effects (positive and negative), the existence of natural monopolies, the indivisibility of goods/services, lack of sufficient information and failure to adopt.

External effects, such as technological external effects like noise or environmental pollution, are a commonly discussed point. Responses to external effects usually involve setting up a system of liabilities for the creation of negative external effects.[9] The Coase theorem proposes setting up a negotiation system which enables all market participants to negotiate over the right to, for example, pollute. To give an example, as a result, fishermen would negotiate with a chemical industry enterprise over the right to pollute water. If the chemical industry is more profitable than the fishermen, they would buy the pollution rights and therefore compensate the fishermen for their losses and vice versa. In the end, there would be no regulation needed, because transactions between market participants and liability rules automatically lead to a welfare optimal point.

Another economic approach to regulation is the Pigou tax or Pigou aid. The Pigou tax is a tax which is imposed on the creator of negative external effects. Its size shall be so that it is generating exactly the revenue that is necessary to make up for the harm represented by the negative external effect. The size of Pigou tax is

---

[6]See Engel and Morlok (1998); van Aken (2004), pp. 1–32; Furubotn and Richter (2010); Homann and Suchanek (2005); Denkhaus (2004), pp. 33–60.

[7]For more information on the desirable market result according to economists, see the comprehensive body of literature on the Pareto criterium e.g. Pareto (1906).

[8]See Hayek (1969).

[9]Positive external effects are not considered. They are assumed to be a by-product which is a neat positive development.

determined according to its ability to generate exactly the revenue that is necessary to make up for the harm represented by the negative external effect.[10]

The indivisibility is acknowledging the fact that some production factors cannot be divided. Another frequently used description for this is a natural monopoly. Natural monopolies are monopolies that occur in markets in which the costs for infrastructure are so high that it is only efficient for one enterprise to operate on a market. If there were more than one enterprise, prices would increase significantly. This occurs when the initial investment (or capital cost) that has to be made is very high and the marginal costs arising from the operating and distribution systems are very low, for example, the low costs of fresh water distribution. According to the concept of subadditivity, it is cheaper for one enterprise to supply a good by the term subadditivity. Additionally, the high initial investment which cannot be reversed, and which therefore is considered a sunk cost represents a barrier to entry for potential competitors on a market.

In Fig. 2.1 given the average costs (AC), marginal costs (MC) and demand (D), it is not viable for more than one enterprise to engage in market. Given that each firm serves half of the total demand, two enterprises would already be unable to cover their costs and therefore would be unable to operate successfully in the market.

Given that enterprises have a tendency to maximize profits and that the profit maximizing point is where marginal revenue (the additional income generated by producing another unit, MR) and marginal costs (the costs for generating another unit) are equal, without regulation, the monopolist would set the monopoly quantity Q_m and receive the monopoly price p_m, another strategy would be to use price differentiation and charge a price that represents every customer's willingness to pay.

In contrast, economic price theory assumes that the most efficient price is the one at which the marginal cost intersects with the demand curve. This price would generate losses for the natural monopolist. There are four concepts which propose how to deal with those losses. The first concept proposes to force the natural monopolist to set the price p_e and the state would compensate the natural monopolist for its losses. This proposal would distribute the financial burden on all members of the state including who are not using it. The second concept allows the natural monopolist to set p_c that is covering the costs. The shortcoming with this concept is that it might be an incentive for the natural monopolist to be less efficient. Surely, it is no incentive at all for the company to reduce the average costs, if the prescribed price is adjusted afterwards. The third concept suggests that the state should take those sectors over and operate them. This idea has the shortcoming that the state might not have an incentive to operate efficiently and be innovative. The fourth concept states that there could be an auction for the right to operate on the natural monopoly market. This approach seems appealing, but it contains many details that would not be able to be covered in contracts. Maintenance duties and the

[10]See Endres (1994); Eskeland (1994), pp. 373–394; Ebert (1991/1992), pp. 154–166; Hurwicz (1995), pp. 49–74; Kahneman et al. (1990), pp. 1325–1348.

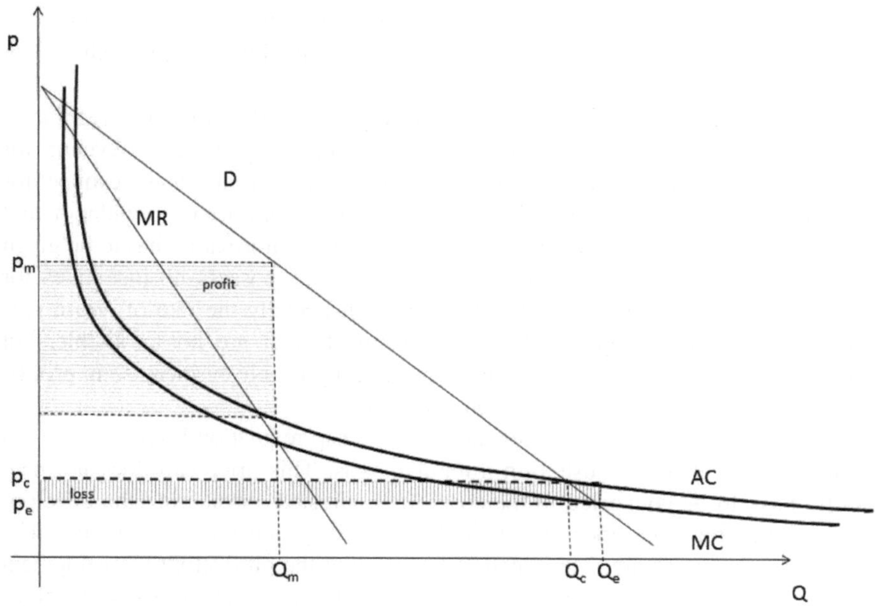

Fig. 2.1 Profits of the natural monopolist. *Source* Own design

quality of the services and products provided are especially difficult to monitor. As a result, the fourth concept also has its shortcomings. Natural monopolies frequently occur in network industries. These industries require significant investment into building the net and the demand is not high enough to establish two competing nets, e.g. a second set of pipes in the ground for water supply. Technically speaking, the net operator owns a crucial, so called "bottleneck", factor for an industry. This could lead to the net operator closing down net access for competitors and consequently establishing a monopoly on all stages of the supply chain.

Therefore, there are new approaches when it comes to the regulation of networks. One approach is cost-plus-regulation (CPR). Enterprises receive a compensation that covers their average cost and adds revenue to it. With this given prices every enterprise can reduce their costs or increase their efficiency or innovation level in order to increase their profits.[11] In the next year, the price is again calculated by the regulator based on the costs of the previous year. This system has been considered very successfully by some economists.[12] Others are critical of it, because the model focuses solely on the reduction of cost and does not contain any

[11]See Lyon (1996), pp. 227–247; Dehmel (2011).

[12]See Schmalensee (1989), pp. 417–436; Niemeier (2002), pp. 37–48.

leeway for searching for innovative solutions and very different set-ups to improve the product or reduce costs, since a budget for this kind of research is not available.[13]

Another regulatory means is rate of return regulation. Rate of return regulation allows enterprises to set prices that cover costs, include additional revenue for business risks that have been undertaken and also include a return on investment for the capital involved in the production.[14] For both tools, the price cap regulation and the rate of return regulation, a large amount of business information has to be given to regulation authorities.[15] Nevertheless, these systems possess no incentives for enterprises to increase efficiency or lower costs. Especially the rate of return regulation might lead to capital intensive investments that are not profitable, but increase the gross revenue numbers and consequently enable an increase in profits. This phenomenon is called Averch-Johnson-Effect.[16]

In addition, there is price cap regulation. Price cap regulation involves setting a maximum price that is adjusted on a regular basis. This price cap does not necessarily have to be connected to the costs. It is adjusted considering the development of general consumer prices and assumed productivity increases. The productivity increases are determined by monitoring the productivity development of an economic sector as a whole. Still, there are shortcomings in this approach as well. Firstly, it is difficult to determine the frequency of the price adjustments. Secondly, it is difficult to track which productivity increases are a result of lower quality.[17]

A lack of sufficient information is another facet of market failure. In such cases, market participants are unaware of the price differences and make irrational decisions they would not have made had they been fully informed. Regulation economics focuses primarily on the challenge of distinguishing high quality from low quality and estimating risks. Regulation economics also focuses on the challenges consumers face when comparing current prices for homogenous goods, as well as their unwillingness and inability to compare them and make a rational decision (which according to economists if to choose buying for the lowest price). In order to respond to this means of market failure, systems are established to facilitate access to important information and inform consumers about them.[18]

In summary, regulation practices have to weigh the costs and benefits against each other. In order to regulate efficiently, there are cost-benefit-analyses conducted before a regulatory act is implemented. Furthermore, the estimated costs of

---

[13]See Crew and Kleindorfer (1996), pp. 211–225.

[14]See Taggart (1981), pp. 383–393; Solomon (1970), pp. 65–81; Sherman (1977), pp. 240–248.

[15]See Liston (1993), pp. 25–48; Pint (1992), pp. 564–578.

[16]See Averch and Johnson (1962), pp. 1052–1069; Spann (1974), pp. 38–52; Bailey and Coleman (1971), pp. 278–292.

[17]See Brunekreeft (2003), Chap. 4 Price-cap regulation; Cabral and Riordan (1989), pp. 93–102; Braeutigam and Panzar (1993), pp. 191–198; Cowan (2002), pp. 167–188.

[18]See Healy and Palepu (2001), pp. 405–440; Acharya et al. (2009), pp. 89–137; Nicolaides (1992), pp. 113–121.

regulatory legislation in particular and legislation in general are conducted. This estimation can be conducted prior to passing regulation, in the process of creating legislation or after the implementation of regulatory legislation. Additionally, network industries are not longer considered to be indivisible and only manageable as a whole. An approach to counter shortcomings of network industries is the essential-facilities doctrine. The essential-facilities doctrine abolished a number of natural monopolies and increased efficiency. This came along with a significant increase in regulation economics approaches how to increase competition and consequently efficiency as well as total welfare. The tools that have been developed accordingly are presented in the legal section.

2.1.3 Sector Specific Regulation

With regards to sector specific regulation, there are some rationales that are share among different sectors and some points that are exclusively used in one or few sectors. Consequently, the following section will explain commonalities in sector specific regulation (Sect. 2.1.3.1) and special characteristics of sector specific regulation (Sect. 2.1.3.2). These special characteristics of sector specific regulation strengthen the different approaches and needs for regulatory actions of sectors that have unique characteristics and function very differently.

2.1.3.1 Commonalities in Sector Specific Regulation

Economic sectors are functioning differently and are each operating in a different economic environment. As a result of this, there is sector specific regulation drafted. The institutional set up of sector specific regulation can also differ among countries. Some countries have one common regulation agency for several network industries like water supply, energy distribution (e.g. the Federal German Network Agency in Germany). Other countries have separated regulatory agencies for different branches (e.g. the UK Office of Communication (Ofcom), the UK Office of Rail and Road (ORR), the Office of the Gas and Electricity Markets (Ofgem), the Water Services Regulation Authority (Ofwat) that are all operating in the United Kingdom). A country can also have a different institutional set-up for the regulation of different industries. An example for this would be a common regulation agency for network industries and specialised regulation agencies for other industrial fields. Furthermore, there can be centralised regulation agencies, decentralised regulation agencies or a sophisticated set up of Federal and state-level regulation agencies.

Additionally, there are aims all sector specific regulators share and that should be secured in all network sectors. The first aim is the provision of net access. This aim is rooted in the essential-facilities-doctrine which states that there are conditions under which enterprises do not have the freedom to refrain from doing business with another enterprise or not allow an enterprise to use a net.[19] These conditions are

- a high market share and consequently a strong market power,
- a lack of factual reasons to refrain from doing business,
- the prevention of competition as a result of denying market access.[20]

Other sector specific regulatory aim or tool is the universal service obligation.[21] Some network sectors require high investments into infrastructure and therefore economically allow only one operator on the market (compare natural monopolies). If an enterprise receives the right to operate, maintain and charge for the usage of this infrastructure, it is not possible to shutdown less lucrative parts and for example stop distributing water in sparsely populated areas.

In case of natural monopolies, there are additional legal obligations for the pricing decision of the enterprise being the natural monopolist. The profit of the natural monopolist is often limited by regulatory acts. Besides that, it is often prohibited to charge to low prices and consequently engage in predatory or limit pricing.

The last core aspects of sector specific regulation are organisational and procedural aspects. The level of independence from political influence is another crucial factor in the institutional set-up of regulation agencies.[22] Regulation agencies are (in democratic market economies) expected to work in order to achieve the regulatory goals which would in turn result in more competitive markets, lower prices, higher consumer and aggregated welfare. Unlike that, the idea of sectorial regulation is not the political management of an industry or single enterprises.[23] Consequently, regulation authorities have to have independent departments for the legal proceedings or ruling chambers.

In conclusion, there are sector specific regulation tools that share some common aims. Nevertheless, it depends on the exact economic environment which set of tools shall be used in a particular sector. These tools will be explained in greater length and detail in the following sections.

[19]See Fritsch (2011), pp. 198 ff.

[20]See Lipsky and Sidak (1998), pp. 1187–1248; Bergman (2001), pp. 403–434; Kezsbom and Goldman (1996), pp. 1–36; Soma et al. (1998), pp. 565–614.

[21]This is especially applicable for postal services and the telecommunications sector, see Gabrisch (1996); Elsenbast (1999).

[22]See Égert (2009); Smith (1997).

[23]See Montoya and Trillas (2009), pp. 113-134; Stern (1997), pp. 67–74.

2.1.3.2 Special Characteristics of Sector Specific Regulation

Still, there are sector specific nuances when it comes to aims of sector regulation. Regulation in the media sector primarily aims at supplying the population with a broad and diverse variety of information on democratic and cultural issues. This constitutes a prerequisite to enable all citizens to make up their mind in political questions and to guarantee forums for the articulation of (diverging) political views on issues. As a result of this the citizens are well informed about global as well as European and domestic politics. Other regulatory aims like the provision of a sufficient infrastructure, competition (and in case of the media sector plurality), the promotion of innovation are also applicable in the media sector.[24]

University regulation is also focusing on a more diverse set of aims. Competition among universities does play a role in university regulation. As a result of competition national champions are expected to ensure competitiveness with universities of other countries Nevertheless, providing access to higher education is still a crucial task. One particular aspect of this is the vocational training and preparation for the labour market after graduation. That is why, one could argue in favour of a universal service obligation for universities to provide education throughout the whole country for everybody who is qualified to pursue university studies. This comes along with a sophisticated set of quality management processes. Still the academic freedom is a limit to public interference with, in this case public regulation of, universities.[25]

Competition is playing a minor role in waste management regulation. The predominant aims in this economic sector are safe disposal and a set of environmental protection aims.[26] Besides that, there shall be incentives to avoid the production of waste and to increase recycling. In the field of waste management, essential facilities (access to sanitary landfills and waste incineration plants) are of crucial importance. Waste management also comes along with a universal service obligation to secure waste management also in rather remote areas. To facilitate waste disposal, there are comprehensive take-back obligations of producers of (especially) electronics.[27]

Financial markets are a unique sector for regulation, because there are no networks connected to the financial sector. Still there are special regulations for financial markets to ensure their existence and to protect the trust of consumers into them. These aims are ensure by two tools, namely the solvency supervision and the protection of the functioning of the markets. The solvency supervision is protecting the money of the savers in case of a major economic crisis. As a result of the global financial crisis 2007–2009, the shares of deposits of banks have been increased and

[24]See Kamps (2006), pp. 133–142; Benz (1997), pp. 419–537; Holznagel et al. (2008).

[25]See Battis and Kersten (2003), pp. 349-357; Ladeur (2005), pp. 753–764; Schmidt-Assmann (1993), pp. 697–711.

[26]See Rockholz (2001); Rutkowsky (1998).

[27]See Behrendt et al. (1996), pp. 114–115.

there were sophisticated regulation for the risk management systems of financial institutions. The protection of the functioning of the markets is emphasising the protection of the financial system at all. But establishing rules for the business conduct on the financial markets, these operations come into being. Without rules for these transactions, they would not take place at all. Apart from the two major aims; combating money laundering is also an aim of the regulation of financial markets.[28]

The universal service obligation is also a crucial part of the health care regulation. Apart from that, there is a sophisticated system of actors who are interacting with each other frequently. Therefore a system of general practitioners, specialised doctors, hospitals and specialised hospitals is established to be able to treat a diverse set of illnesses for a high number of patients within a short period of time. Consequently, quality management and overall coverage is more important than competition on the health care sector. Still, the health care system is moving into a direction of incentives to treat patients more efficiently. These incentives are also including bonus-malus-systems for patients who take care for their health. To avoid cherry picking and refraining from insuring people with pre-existing conditions, most health care regulations are having sophisticated legal provisions to prevent these patterns.[29]

The aim of postal regulation, apart from the universal service obligation, is to protect the secrecy of letters and data protection as well as enabling all citizens to use postal services at an affordable price. Nevertheless, competition is becoming a major concern in postal regulation.[30]

Water supply regulation also roots in the universal service obligation. But there are more aspects to the issue. Sanitary aspects of providing clean water are just as important as the maintenance of the infrastructure. Furthermore, there are market behaviour and market entry regulations that ensure the protection of the water quality.[31]

Energy regulation, telecommunications regulation and railway regulation can be summarized under the aspects of net regulation with only a minor importance of quality management tools. The primary focus of these sectors is providing access for possible competitors and trying to work as efficiently as possible. Additionally, those sectors are facing some fees regulations.[32]

---

[28]See Kümpel and Wittig (2011); Follak (1986).

[29]See Kingreen (2005), pp. 505–511.

[30]See Gärditz (2005), pp. 490–497; Wieland (1995), pp 315 ff.

[31]See Besche (2004); Forster (2007).

[32]See Boysen et al. (2007).

2.1.4 *Constitutional Limits and Obligations of Regulation*

Legal amendments have to take place while respecting constitutional limits for regulatory actions. Therefore an overview on regulation law and regulation economics also needs to consider the constitutional limits of regulation. Furthermore the constitution can also justify state interference with a market. Therefore, this section outlines the limits of regulation when it comes to the issue of professional freedom (Sect. 2.1.4.1), the freedom of property (Sect. 2.1.4.2), the general freedom of actions (Sect. 2.1.4.3), the principle of equality (Sect. 2.1.4.4); the principle of proportionality (Sect. 2.1.4.5) and the national objectives and national structural principles (Sect. 2.1.4.6), the application of fundamental rights to enterprises (Sect. 2.1.4.7). The assessment does not just consider domestic German legal norms, but also obligations from EU law (Sect. 2.1.4.8), from the European Convention of Human Rights (Sect. 2.1.4.9) and from other international law sources (Sect. 2.1.4.10).

2.1.4.1 Professional Freedom

According to Art. 12 GG, professional freedom is protected by the German constitution. Professional freedom contains two major elements, the freedom to choose one's profession and the freedom to exercise one's profession. Nevertheless, professional freedom is subject to legal reservation and can be limited by law to a certain extent.[33]

The good that is subject to protection is the freedom to choose a job, an education and the freedom to start a business in a particular field. That includes the freedom to contract external parties and the freedom to set prices. Additionally, business secrets are protected from being released. Because many professions require sophisticated skills and knowledge, there are a significant amount of laws that restrict professional freedom. Regulatory measures could limit professional freedom by obliging people and enterprises to do some steps or refrain from doing so.

In order to properly protect professional freedom despite all restrictions, the Federal German Constitutional Court developed a system that includes a three step assessment. The first step is the way and means of how the freedom to exercise one's profession is restricted. In those cases, the interest of the general public has to be weighed against unproportional regulations. An example of this would be limiting the opening hours of shops in the middle of the night. The second step is dealing with the question of whether or not the restriction of professional freedom is based on subjective access requirements e.g. certain qualifications etc. The third step is the question of whether or not there is a restriction of professional freedom on objective admission criteria. This is the most severe impact and the measure

[33]See Hufen (1994), pp. 2913–2921.

which affects the fundamental rights the most. Examples of this are quotas for pharmacies or the admission system for the access to university studies in medicine.[34]

A significant number of measures interfere with professional freedom, namely unbundling, net access questions, the universal service obligation and price regulation. Nevertheless, the state can engage in those issues as there are several reasons why the state is allowed to intervene.[35] Technically speaking, a law or regulation which limits a fundamental rights or freedom, this is also applicable to all of the following fundamental rights and freedoms, has to outline in its text the fact that it is limiting a fundamental freedom or right and has to name it, according to Art. 19 (1) GG.

2.1.4.2 Freedom of Property

According to Art. 14 GG, freedom of property is protected by the German constitution. It primarily protects the private benefit of property, as well as the power of deposition of the property owner with regards to one's property.

Regulation law may interfere with freedom of property if the power of deposition of the property is restricted because of measures like a universal service obligations and the right to net access. Nevertheless, the constitutional barriers for regulation with special emphasis on freedom of property are low, because of the social use obligation of property.

The freedom of property is also closely interlinked with the freedom of action. In many cases it is difficult to impossible to distinguish whether or not one or the other is primarily applicable. This is important, because the legal consequence of limiting the freedom of property is the obligation to provide compensation.

At the same time, freedom of property according to Art. 14 GG also emphasizes the importance of social obligations that come along with property. Consequently, the protection of individual interests does not allow property owners to conduct business in whichever way they prefer.[36]

If the protection of individual freedom becomes less important, there is plenty of leeway for regulators to interfere in market environments they consider anti-competitive or those which have a high potential for welfare increases as a result of regulation.

Art. 14 (3) GG additionally outlines the possibility for expropriation. This tool is the ultima ratio for the legislative body. That is unlikely to be the case for regulation

---

[34]See Federal German Constitutional Court Decisions 7, 377; 13, 97; 13, 181; 19, 337; 28, 374; 33, 125; 33, 303; 39, 225; 54, 301; 82, 209; 93, 235.

[35]See Badura (2003), pp. 785–800; Wollenschläger (2013), pp. 7–16.

[36]See Riedel (2012).

authorities, because regulation authorities strive to enable competition among private actors and to revive a market.[37]

2.1.4.3 General Freedom of Actions

The general freedom of actions may be cited as an additional obstacle for regulatory measures. Compared to the freedom of equity and the freedom of property, the general freedom of actions, Art. 2 GG is a vague concept. Art. 2 GG is assessed subsidiarily. If specific fundamental rights or freedoms are not applicable, the general freedom of actions may pose a constitutional limit. Furthermore, it covers positive and negative actions and therefore the choice of an enterprise to refrain from doing something e.g. forwarding information.

In the case at hand, economic freedom may be limited by regulatory means with the intention of creating a more efficient and competitive economy. Limiting the general freedom of actions is possible when it is done by a proper law (see introductory remarks above). Furthermore, somebody else's freedom of actions should not be affected when exercising one's own freedom of actions. Another limit is that the moral law of a society should be respected when exercising one's freedom of action.

2.1.4.4 Principle of Equality

Another fundamental right that might limit regulatory measures is the principle of equality. According to the principle of equality established in Art. 3 GG, equal groups have to be treated equally and unequal groups have to be treated unequally. This norm is crucial for all administrative actions.

Taking this rational into consideration, similar industrial sectors have to be treated equally. This rational is originally derived from the prohibition of arbitrary procedures. Therefore, different regulatory tools in different economic sectors have to be justified. Additionally, this concept also states that regulatory actions that treat different groups of persons or enterprises differently have to be subject to detailed explanations.[38]

2.1.4.5 Principle of Proportionality

A core aspect when passing and implementing regulatory measures is the principle of proportionality. The principle of proportionality is not itself mentioned in the German Basic Law, but it is a core component of the rule of law that is enshrined in

[37]See Möllinger (2009).

[38]See Altwicker (2011), pp. 364–378.

Art. 20 (3) GG. It states that fundamental rights and fundamental freedoms are not without limits. The Federal State is allowed to limit them in accordance with the principle of proportionality.

That is why all regulatory means have to have a (1) legitimate purpose. If fundamental rights or freedoms are limited, there has to be a legitimate purpose to do that. Regulation law usually states consumer welfare, the protection of competition on markets and related points as justification for its actions. Furthermore, the regulatory means have to be (2) suitable to achieve this particular goal. Additionally, there has to be a (3) necessity for those particular regulatory means. In order to affirm that, there must not be any mean that is less severe and would achieve the same goal to the same degree. Finally, the application of those regulatory means has to be (4) appropriate. When evaluating the appropriation of regulatory means, the effects of the reduction of the fundamental rights or fundamental freedoms are weighed against the positive effects for e.g. consumer welfare or market competition.

In conclusion, every interference with fundamental rights and fundamental freedoms that occurs within the process of regulation has to consider the principle of proportionality. If all four aspects are assessed positively, namely there is a legitimate purpose, the regulatory means are suitable, there is a necessity for the use of this particular mean and the application is appropriate, a measure can be considered proportional. This tool is the major criteria to answer the question whether or not fundamental rights and freedoms that have been described in the previous parts of this section can be limited.

2.1.4.6 National Objectives and National Structural Principles

National objectives refer to aims a state intends to achieve. Because of their significance, they are laid out in the constitution of the state. The national structural principles of the German Basic law (Art. 20 GG) are the establishment and maintenance of the welfare state, the protection of democracy, the maintenance of a federal system, and the separation of power and the rule of law, environmental protection and additional protective duties. These protective duties include the protection of health, life and physical integrity as a whole as well as the protection of marriage and the family. The social welfare state is often mentioned in combination with the prohibition to discriminate on the grounds of sex, ethnic origin, race, language, belief, political ideology and disability.

Additional national objectives are achieving macro-economic equilibrium[39] and participation in European integration[40] and international cooperation.[41] There are still minimal procedural tools to ensure national objectives are considered in the

[39]Art. 109 (2) GG.

[40]Art. 23 (1) GG.

[41]Art. 24 GG.

law-making and regulatory process. Most national objectives are tools which allow law-makers to appease interest groups by highlighting their significance in the constitution.

. Some national objectives and structural principles are more applicable when assessing regulation than others. The principle of democracy is a main tool when it comes to the accountability of regulatory decisions. Consequently, democratic legitimacy is a crucial limitation for the regulatory process. Another crucial factor is the rule of law in all regulatory processes. That is why legal proceedings against regulatory decisions and regulatory processes have to be possible. Other national objectives include outlining the visionary framework according to which regulatory measures are a means to an end. Because they can be perceived as part of the set of aims for regulation, they do not need to be further assessed as potential limits.

2.1.4.7 Application of Fundamental Rights to Enterprises

Fundamental rights as well as national objectives often apply to individual people when protecting themselves against regulation. Nevertheless, there are many enterprises or legal persons that might be subject to regulatory acts.

Art 19 (3) GG protects enterprises to a certain degree from public interference and makes them subjects of fundamental rights. This idea is not an anomaly of the fundamental rights idea. Art. 19 (3) GG was created to protect individuals that formed organisations.

According to Art. 19(3) GG, fundamental rights and freedoms protect enterprises against unjustified and disproportional interference of regulation agencies and other public entities to a certain degree. The fundamental rights and freedoms have to be able to apply to the characteristics of legal persons in general or enterprises in particular. As a result, enterprises cannot claim to circumvent merger regulation by stating the freedom of marriage or the protection of the family. However, enterprises do still enjoy freedom of property, professional freedom and equality.

2.1.4.8 Obligations from EU Law

The European law also contains a number of restrictions for regulation law. These restrictions are laid out in the treaties on the European Union (EU), TEU und TFEU. Since Germany is part of the EU, its treaties and legal norms are binding and directly applicable.[42] Art. 23 GG emphasises the importance of European integration. This significance also includes the importance of EU legal norms that are superior to domestic German law. Therefore, EU legal norms need to be considered when defining constitutional limits of regulation.

[42]See ECJ, Case 26/62 van Gend en Loos.

Art. 2 TEU guarantees equality amongst the people. This refers primarily to equality in front of a court, but also includes equal treatment for the same people. Furthermore, freedom is protected by Art. 2 TEU. Nevertheless, both concepts are not explained in more details. Therefore, the effect this has on regulation law remains unclear. ... The significant reduction of one's freedom or the different treatment of similar people, cases or industries can still be considered a breach of European law.

Additionally, Art. 3 TEU establishes the common European market. Therefore, regulatory measures must not harm the establishment of a common European market. As a result, regulatory means must have the same effect for domestic as well as other European products, services and investments.

Other norms such as Art. 4 (2) lit. e TFEU environmental protection, Art. 4 (2) lit. f TFEU consumer protection, Art. 6 lit. a TFEU human also represent potential limits for regulatory activities. These norms are still vague when compared to the obligations from the German GG. Furthermore, claimants would rather consider the fundamental rights and freedoms from the GG as opposed to those from European law.

2.1.4.9 Obligations from the European Convention of Human Rights

As a party to the European Convention of Human Rights (ECHR), Germany has to organize its regulation in accordance with the convention. Nevertheless, the main focus of the ECHR is political rights. Economic freedom rights or economic rights in general are not the focus. Furthermore, there are no duties in the ECHR that have not already been outlined in the GG or the EU treaties.

If domestic German courts do not manage to properly protect fundamental rights and freedoms and if the European Court of Justice (ECJ) does not protect them by preliminary ruling, the European Court of Human Rights can be called to protect them. Accordingly, there are no additional duties in the ECHR. The ECHR simply represents another instance or tool for people to demand their rights and freedoms to be protected.

2.1.4.10 Obligations from Other International Law Sources

According to Art. 24 GG, international law is superior to German legal acts. Furthermore, it is generally applicable and has direct effect for German citizens. Because of the predominant position of the idea of sovereignty, there are little obligations from public international law. International economic law is still highly relevant in the assessment of limits for regulatory measures. In the field of economic law, WTO law and bi- or plurilateral trade and/or investment treaties are important.[43]

[43] See Ginsburg (2005), pp. 107–123.

When drafting regulation, the core WTO principle of national treatment has to be considered. According to the principle of national treatment, foreign and domestic products must be treated equally. As a result, regulation which favours domestic products over foreign products is prohibited.

Bi- or plurilateral trade and/or investment treaties may represent an additional limit for regulation. Trade and investment treaties usually contain a clause that prevents the legislator from making major legislative changes to the domestic environment. Art XX GATT could possibly serve as a legal framework to determine circumstances under which it is allowed to restrict trade or investments. These are namely, (a) the protection of public morals, (b) the protection of human, animal and plant life and health etc. They do not mention the protection of the competitiveness of markets, small and medium-sized competitors or consumer welfare as a justification for limiting trade. As a result, bilateral or plurilateral trade or investment agreements represent a limit for regulation.

2.2 Legal Aspects of Vertical Integration

With the state interfering with free markets, there are a number of policy aims and an even broader variety of tools which are used in order to achieve a politically desired market result. Consequently, a number of regulatory aims and tools need to be presented in greater length and are later evaluated in order to assess the impact vertical integration has. Some aspects do not solely fall into a legal or economic category. Therefore they are added to the category which they affect most. This does not necessarily mean that they do not at all can be located also in the economic or legal field as well.

Still at first, the phenomenon of vertical integration is presented and the dissenting assessments of it are presented (Sect. 2.2.1). In order to compensate for negative and strengthen positive aspects of vertical integration, a number of legal tools are presented in greater detail. Among the legal aspects, (possible) regulation tools are presented, namely unbundling regulations (Sect. 2.2.2), the right to net access (Sect. 2.2.3), regulation of capacity shortages (Sect. 2.2.4), transparency regulations (Sect. 2.2.5), market access regulations (Sect. 2.2.6), as well as market behaviour regulations (Sect. 2.2.7).

2.2.1 General Regulation

The key argument for regulation law is based on the idea that by allowing the invisible hand to determine equilibrium we are unable to provide results that are sufficient and welfare optimizing for society as a whole.

Apart from natural monopolies where competition is impossible, regulation strives to use market mechanisms to determine equilibriums. Regulation also adds particular legal requirements in order to achieve political goals as well.

Regulation sectors can be divided in the economic sector (networks, media, social affairs and the environment) or according to the regulation aims. The aim can be to ensure and protect competition, to increase efficiency in a market, to provide safety and security, to preserve the environment, to protect public service and to ensure a proper liability of suppliers towards their customers.

Vertical integration has been a highly disputed economic phenomenon and the scientific community is ambiguous on how to perceive and therefore how to deal with it. One position is welcoming vertical integration, because of its efficiency effects and the elimination of double marginalisation.[44] The other position is criticising vertical integration, because of the increased options to harm non-vertically integrated competitors.[45]

2.2.2 *Unbundling Regulations/Disintegration Regulations*

Another legal regulation tool of unbundling is the disintegration of an enterprise. This tool can be used in three different ways. Its aim is to avoid the cross-subsidization of particular sectors or single steps as part of the supply chain. Traditional unbundling stems from the separation of providing a net and operating it. There are already a number of sector specific laws regarding public transportation, the transportation of goods via railways or energy distribution. Outside of net sectors, unbundling is used to prevent the distortion of competition. The general aim is to provide goods and/or services in an efficient way and serve the general interest by doing so.[46]

There are two approaches of how to avoid this problem. There can be accounting separation (Sect. 2.2.2.1) or organisational separation (Sect. 2.2.2.2).

2.2.2.1 Accounting Separation

Accounting separation is a tool used to assign costs. When costs are clearly assigned to individual business operations, other regulations like the prohibition of margin squeeze can be implemented properly. Furthermore, accounting separation helps to compensate enterprises properly for the costs of maintaining and expanding an existing net structure.

---

[44]See Gugler et al. (2017), pp. 450–478.

[45]See Acemoglu and Johnson (2005), pp. 949–995; Doidge et al. (2007), pp. 1–39; Claessens and Yurtoglu (2013), pp. 1–33.

[46]See Pollitt (2008), pp. 704–713; Steiner (2000), Jamasb and Pollitt (2005), pp. 11–41.

The special challenges of accounting separation are, however, how to deal with fixed costs. Furthermore, it is difficult to prevent informal coordination by the enterprise itself, because the factual independence of the enterprise's operations as a whole is difficult to achieve. Still, accounting separation could serve as a tool to create a framework for competition.[47]

2.2.2.2 Organisational Separation

The organisational separation of an enterprise has different degrees. It has its roots in the distinction between the operation of the net and using the net for one's own business affairs. Apart from avoiding cross-subsidization of other company operations, organisational separation prevents integrated enterprises that do not grant (fair) access to a particular market.[48]

Organisational separation already is a very deeply reaching regulatory tool. It comes along with major structural changes rather than simply minor policy modifications. Still organisational separation usually does not include a transfer of ownership and is therefore different from the traditional unbundling idea. Nevertheless, unbundling could be a further step in the process of organisational separation.

2.2.3 Net Access

Denying net access to fringe firms[49] is a way in which dominant and vertically integrated enterprises can prevent competition. Net access obligations allow competition on markets which would otherwise have a natural monopoly. In order to prevent major firms from excluding possible competitors by excluding them from net access, regulatory bottlenecks are created that put particular burdens on a dominant firm on how to use its property, namely the net. That is why two regulatory practices regarding net access are presented. Firstly, the right to net access is outlined (Sect. 2.2.3.1). Secondly, regulation regarding fees is presented (Sect. 2.2.3.2).

2.2.3.1 Right to Net Access

Net access is a crucial element in the case of natural monopolies. By providing the infrastructure and allowing competitors to enter the market, competition is

[47]See Cave and Martin (1994), pp. 12–20.

[48]See Cave (2007), pp. 89–103.

[49]Usually the term "enterprise" is used. In this particular circumstance the term "fringe firms" is used as a technical term.

stimulated. Otherwise, competitors would not enter the market, because they would be afraid of sunk costs (irreversible costs which cannot be compensated when leaving a market, strong economies of scale and scope by the dominant firm[50] on a particular market). Especially net sectors like telecommunications, energy and railways are affected by the obligation to grant net access to competitors.

Consequently, these bottlenecks are regulated to enable enterprises to enter the market as fringe firms without the burden of setting up a network, but the privilege of using one. In contrast, the right to net access can be suspended in order to reward and protect high investments into nets. This is referred to by the term "regulatory vacation".[51]

There is a special regulation for the telecommunications sector in place. According to the approach of "asymmetrical regulation", enterprises with a particular degree of market power have to grant net access to those enterprises without this level of market power.

Crucial points in net access are situations with capacity or usage conflicts. The property point of view clearly states that an enterprise's own downstream operations would be supplied first. However, this contradicts with the prohibition of discrimination of competitors.[52]

2.2.3.2 Fees for Net Access

The regulation of net access also needs to cover the regulation of fees for net access, because it is often difficult to distinguish which costs occur at which level. Without a regulation of fees for net access, the prohibition of discrimination could not be monitored properly and could consequently not be implemented. As a result of this failure, enterprises might be unable enter a market, because the fees for net access are making it impossible to compete on a market due to the cost disadvantage. There are two main approaches to monitoring the fees for net access, namely "Ramsey pricing" and "price cap regulation".

Ramsey pricing is the traditional approach which considers the costs of building, maintaining and operating a net and adds a particular profit margin to it. The approach considers the total costs. Nevertheless, there is little incentive to improve the system, because the profit margin remains the same. At the same time, it is very difficult to estimate an efficient price when there is a lack of a market which could lead to this efficient result. The price cap regulation is outlining a maximum price for net access fees.[53]

[50]Usually the term "enterprise" is used. In this particular circumstance the term "dominant firm" is used as a technical term.

[51]See Baumol et al. (1983), pp. 491–496; Scholtka (2005), pp. 2421–2425.

[52]See Storr (2006), pp. 1017–1026.

[53]See Säcker (2009), pp. 78–85; Brunekreeft (2003).

2.2.4 Regulation of Capacity Shortages

In order to protect competition in a market with a high degree of vertical integration, the regulation of capacity shortages is a crucial aspect to be examined. Some courts denied an obligation of the network operator to expand the network in case of capacity shortages.[54] Consequently, every (potential) market entrant has to take over financial burdens related to the net expansion, if it desires to enter the market.[55]

2.2.5 Transparency Regulations

The concept of perfect competition or perfectly competitive markets is heavily relying on price transparency. Consequently, transparency regulations could play a major role for the protection or enablement of competition. §47a ff. German Act against Restraints of Competition (GWB) is providing the legal basis for an assessment of the pricing behaviour of enterprises. With those data, prohibited market behaviour can be investigated.

According to §47k GWB, price data can also be made available to final consumers via consumer information services. This information is intended to facilitate the price comparison and allow consumers to pick the cheapest price for homogenous goods.[56]

2.2.6 Market Entry Regulation

Market entry regulations are not traditionally rooted in regulation law, but are rather a tool of commercial law. They justification usually is the reliability of the enterprise attempting to enter the market. According to the sector that is investigated, these tools differ from area to area.

In case of public transportation, railway and road transportation, security reasons are the main concern for market access regulation. Besides that, protecting or enabling a broad variety of choices or areas covered is the underlying rational for market entry regulation on the broadcasting as well as the financial or health sector. Public university have to have new study programmes approved, with many exceptions.[57]

---

[54]See Federal German Administrative Court (2001), pp. 1399–1407.

[55]Knittel (2006), pp. 201–222.

[56]See Semigran et al. (2017), pp. E186–E192; Granados et al. (2010), pp. 207–226.

[57]See Stahler and Upmann (2008), pp. 611–626.

Due to the tendency of deregulation, the paradigm is shifting from market access regulation to a system of access notification. As a result of this, universities have the right to modify their study programmes and simply notify the public administration. The same process took place in the telecommunications sector, the energy supply sector and the sector of additional postal services. The regulation of market entry itself has also been modified in many fields and is organised by e.g. the external accreditation of study programmes or enabling universities to have internal processes of quality management implemented.[58]

2.2.7 Market Behaviour Regulation

A number of other legal regulations can be put in place to stimulate competition in a market with high vertical integration. The legal regulations presented here do not represent an exhaustive list but offer an overview of the main tools.

One market behaviour that is considered harmful for competition is margin squeeze pricing. The prohibition of margin squeeze pricing is a frequent tool to protect small and medium size enterprises in a vertically integrated market. A prohibition of margin squeeze prohibits charging relatively high prices on the wholesale level and relatively low prices on the retail level which make it impossible for enterprises that are only operating on the retail level to compete. There are three different definitions on how a margin squeeze is constituted. They can be called an "absolute" margin squeeze, the equally-efficient test and the reasonably-efficient test.

An absolute margin squeeze is defined by a price on the retail level which is lower than the price on the wholesale level. The equally-efficient test examines whether or not an equally efficient enterprise could (without cross-subsidization) successfully operate on the downstream market (assuming the downstream market is the competitive and the upstream market is highly concentrated) at a particular margin. The reasonably-efficient test examines whether or not an enterprise that is not as efficient, but "reasonably" efficient (possibly without enjoying economies of scale or economies of scope) could successfully operate on the downstream market at a particular margin.[59]

The absolute margin squeeze is the strictest definition, but the one which can be operationalized most easily. Due to a lack of information on costs of an enterprise's

[58]See Pünder (2006), pp. 567–599.

[59]See Crocioni and Veljanovski (2003), pp. 28–60; Heimler (2010), pp. 879–890; Gaudin and Saavedra (2014), pp. 157–172.

downstream operation, a calculation of equally efficient costs is very difficult to do. In addition to that, there is no clear definition of what "reasonably efficient" means and where to draw the line to "unreasonably efficient".[60]

Another legal tool is the prohibition of the abuse of market dominance. This principle is prominently established as a major pillar of the European Union's competition law. It allows for having a dominant market position, but it prohibits its abuse. Consequently, it is not prohibited to become a monopolist. Nevertheless, as a monopolist, there are limits for the monopolist on how to set the price and how much revenue is reasonable. There is a vivid debate about what constitutes an abuse. There are no clear cut criteria that define the element of offence, abuse of market dominance.[61]

In conclusion, the prohibition of market dominance in its current legal form is difficult to operationalize. In general, market behaviour regulations are difficultly implementable.

2.3 Economic Aspects of Vertical Integration

There are a number of legal rules and regulations in the field of vertical integration. Economic theory is also dealing with effects of vertical integration on competitiveness, consumer and overall welfare. The economic aspects of vertical integration include parallel pricing, collusive behaviour and double marginalization. Apart from that, there are other behavioural means which might affect the market result of a highly vertically integrated market.

There is a vivid debate in the scientific community about whether or not vertical integration has an impact at all on consumer prices.[62] The Chicago School was a vocal supporter of an unregulated to little regulated market and saw no negative effect in vertical integration. Nevertheless, the Chicago School reacted to the criticism in the 1960s and developed a more sophisticated view on vertical integration.[63]

The potential or expected effects of vertical integration are presented in the following sections. Firstly, the effect on collusive conduct (Sect. 2.3.1) is presented. Secondly, the elimination of double marginalization (Sect. 2.3.2) is explained. Thirdly, there might be efficiency effects (Sect. 2.3.3) for the vertically integrated enterprise. Fourthly, the potential elimination of competitors (Sect. 2.3.4) as a result

[60]See Carlton (2008), pp. 271–278; Sidak (2008), pp. 279–309; Geradin and O'Donoghue (2005), pp. 355–425; Hou (2014), pp. 43–74.

[61]See Jung (2017), pp. 981–1020.

[62]See Hart and Tirole (1990), p. 205.

[63]For a comprehensive discussion on the effects of vertical integration see Riordan (1998), pp. 1232–1248; Foros and Stehen (2013), pp. 640–661; Hart and Tirole (1990), pp. 205–286; Beard et al. (2001), pp. 319–333; Edwards (1953), pp. 404–410; Riordan and Salop (1995), pp. 513–568; Siegwarth Meyer and Wang (2011), pp. 7–11.

of vertical integration is assessed. Fifthly, the evasion of regulation as a result of vertical integration is presented (Sect. 2.3.5).Lastly, the additional market effects as a result of vertical integration according to economic theory will be analysed (Sect. 2.3.6).

2.3.1 Collusive Conduct

According to oligopoly theory, rational enterprises consider each other's prices (or assumed prices) when making their own pricing decisions. The phenomenon is investigated in the field of game theory.[64] From this point of view, enterprises are expected to collude in specific environmental settings.

Given that the market structure is modified as a result of vertical integration, collusive conduct among enterprises might be facilitated and therefore increase.

There are two main pricing patterns which result from collusive conduct, namely parallel pricing and Edgeworth cycles. Parallel pricing (Sect. 2.3.1.1) is a less controversial indicator of collusive conduct, whereas the occurrence of Edgeworth cycles (Sect. 2.3.1.2) cannot be considered as a clear indicator of collusion.

2.3.1.1 Parallel Pricing

Some characteristics of markets foster collusive behaviour in markets. These characteristics are a high concentration of market shares among a few enterprises, a high market transparency and product homogeneity. These three factors allow for monitoring of the fulfilment of collusive pricing behaviour.

In contrast to price fixing and establishing a cartel, parallel pricing is not an element of offence in any competition law. Rather parallel pricing is a rational decision taken by enterprises to set a duopoly price or to supply the duopoly quantity when there is only one other enterprise in the market and game theory assumes this strategy to be most profitable. Respectively, enterprises are also expected to charge the oligopoly price in the case of more than two market players.[65]

2.3.1.2 Edgeworth Cycles

The debate about the effects of Edgeworth cycles on competition and whether they indicate a lack of competition or a highly competitive market has become commonplace amongst economists.

---

[64]For more information on game theory see Berninghaus et al. (2010); Strategische Spiele: eine Einführung in die Spieltheorie; Rieck (2007); Holler and Illing (2009).

[65]See Devlin (2007), pp. 1111–1151; Watson (1998), pp. 1769–1769; Noel (2016), pp. 287–311.

Edgeworth cycles are pricing pattern which occur in price-sensitive markets. In the beginning, there is price equilibrium in the downstream market. The competing enterprises will lower the prices slightly and always undercut their rivals' prices in order to gain the entire market share. The minimum level for this price decrease is the point at which the price on the downstream market reaches the level on the upstream market. Every enterprise will try to refrain from being the first to increase the price. Finally, one enterprise has to increase the price. Once it does so, all other enterprises follow and the cycle starts again.[66]

Among economists, the occurrence of Edgeworth cycles is an indicator of imperfect markets. Besides that, they are considered to be a form of collusive conduct.

2.3.2 *Double Marginalization*

The first economic argument in favour of vertical integration was the abolishment of double marginalization.[67] Double marginalization describes a situation in which a monopolist on the upstream level (or some superior market level in the course of a supply chain) reaps the monopoly profit, whereas a monopolist on the downstream level sets its own monopoly price, considering the price that was paid on the upstream level. This market structure and market behaviour leads to a higher market price and a lower total welfare compared to the pricing patterns of a vertical integrated enterprise which sets one monopoly price instead of two monopoly prices on two different levels.[68]

This argument was developed against the per se illegality of vertical integration according the US courts in the 1950s. If there were any negative effects on vertically integrated markets, they were assumed to stem from horizontal integration or other sources. Vertical integration was considered as favourable and efficient.[69]

2.3.3 *Efficiency Effects*

The vertical integration of an enterprise might also lead to efficiencies based on the elimination of sales efforts. Other efficiencies can occur based on reduced handling costs. On top of that, the quality of the final product might increase, because the

[66]See Maskin and Tirole (1988), pp. 571–599.

[67]For the first case see Spengler (1950), pp. 347–352.

[68]See Salinger (1988), p. 354; Riordan and Salop (1995), p. 517; Siegwarth Meyer and Wang (2011), p. 8.

[69]See Spengler (1950), p. 352.

vertically integrated enterprise is more closely handling the semi-products which are later sold as the final products by the enterprise.[70]

A high level of efficiency can also have a negative effect. If the enterprises that are vertically integrated are very efficient, they possess significant advantages over all their competitors. By integrating them and consequently combining their efficiencies, they have a significant advantage compared to their competitors. The advantage can be so strong that all other competitors have to leave the market which then in return allows the vertically integrated enterprise to increase prices to the monopoly level.[71] The efficiency gains can also be non-monetary.[72]

2.3.4 *Elimination of Competitors*

Vertical integration might lead to increased market power of the vertically integrated enterprise.[73] There are different ways in which a vertically integrated enterprise might be able to eliminate competitors. In circumstances with a high level of vertical integration, an enterprise might have nearly monopolistic powers or a quasi-monopolistic relationship.[74] The major business conducted to reach this goal include the refusal to supply, as well as preferential supply (Sect. 2.3.4.1), limit pricing as well as predatory pricing (Sect. 2.3.4.2), and price discrimination and raising rivals' costs (Sect. 2.3.4.3).

2.3.4.1 Refusal to Supply and Preferential Supply

Besides that, the vertically integrated enterprise might refuse to supply competitors on the downstream level or provide commodities or semi-finished products primarily to its own downstream operations and limit the supply of others.[75]

The refusal to supply is the main objective which is raised concerning vertical integration. The Chicago School has repeatedly criticized this point. Apart from foreclosing the market for independent competitors, vertically integrated enterprises are more likely to sell intermediate goods to competitors in order to increase efficiency in their own downstream operations.[76] Consequently, Salinger (1988)

---

[70]See Edwards (1953), p. 405; Siegwarth Meyer and Wang (2011), p. 7.

[71]See Hart and Tirole (1990), p. 213; Yamawake et al. (2018), pp. 1028 ff.

[72]See Kim and Nora (2018), pp. 1 ff.

[73]See Edwards (1953), p. 410.

[74]See Footnote 73.

[75]See Edwards (1953), p. 408.

[76]See Salinger (1988), p. 349.

suggests that once the market is not foreclosed for competitors, vertical integration lowers consumer prices and therefore leads to efficient market equilibrium.[77]

On the contrary, Normann (2008) assumes that the vertically integrated enterprise will refrain from selling the intermediate good on the upstream level given Bertrand competition and increase its prices in order to generate more profits on the downstream level. Other competitors will likely increase their prices in order to make more profits. With the increased upstream price, the vertically integrated enterprise will re-enter the upstream market, undercut their competitors' prices and supply the entire market. As a result of this, the equilibrium will not be affected and refusal to supply will not last for a significant time.[78]

Salinger (1988) assumes that vertical integration always leads to lower consumer prices and therefore a higher general welfare if one condition is met. This condition is the prevention of foreclosures by the vertical integration. He considers this aspect crucial in his assessment of vertical integration.[79] There are several economic models that perceive vertical integration as a risk for the foreclosure of markets and/or customers.[80]

2.3.4.2 Limit Pricing and Predatory Pricing

Another economic phenomenon which can occur in vertically highly integrated markets is margin squeeze pricing or predatory pricing. This refers to the vertically integrated enterprise charging high prices on the upstream level and comparatively low prices on the downstream level. Consequently, the downstream market operations of the vertically integrated enterprise have a significant edge over vertically non-integrated enterprises. As a result of this, the non-integrated enterprises can be pushed out of the market which in a final step would allow the vertically integrated enterprise to increase the prices to the monopoly level.[81] In particular, markets with traditional monopolies or a high market concentration bear the risk of this particular type of business conduct.

2.3.4.3 Price Discrimination and Raising Rival Costs

Price discrimination is defined as a pricing behaviour whereby customers pay a different price for the same good or the same price for different goods.

---

[77]See Salinger (1988), p. 355.

[78]See Normann (2008), pp. 7f.

[79]See Footnote 77.

[80]See lately Nocke and Rey (2018), pp. 183 ff.

[81]See Edwards (1953), p. 409.

The vertically integrated enterprise might use its increased bargaining power to charge higher prices on upstream as well as downstream levels.[82]

These pricing strategies can be summarized by the phrase "raising rivals costs" strategies. After a vertical integration, the non-integrated enterprises might have an incentive to counter-merge.[83]

2.3.5 Circumvention of Regulation

Apart from behaviour of integrated enterprises, non-integrated enterprises have a number of different tools to reduce competition using a number of legal or illegal tools. When assessing the effect vertical integration has on competition, it is also necessary to evaluate the alternative option. Therefore, vertical restraints in particular (Sect. 2.3.5.1) and resale price maintenance specifically (Sect. 2.3.5.2) are presented.

2.3.5.1 Vertical Restraints

Further techniques to limit competition of non-integrated enterprises include the establishment of vertical restraints. These vertical restraints can be franchising fees that are usually non-linear, forcing retailers to buy minimum quantities, pricing requirements, tying of products or exclusive territory agreements.[84]

Exclusive territories are perceived as a circumstance that is not welfare optimal.[85] When modelled, exclusive territories show a welfare increase for producers, because they are able to generate higher mark-ups for their products.[86]

Comprehensively analysing the effects of vertical restraints, they decrease competition. The welfare loss by consumers strongly outweighs the welfare gain for producers. Vertical restraints were in particular very effecting for the producers, because they were much easier enforceable than price agreements.[87]

2.3.5.2 Resale Price Maintenance

One means of enterprises is to potentially circumvent regulation and ensure the obedience of standards the introduction of resale price maintenance by being

[82]See Edwards (1953), pp. 406 f.

[83]See Normann (2008), p. 30; Siegwarth Meyer and Wang (2011), p. 7.

[84]See Rey and Stiglitz (1988), p. 1.

[85]See Rey and Stiglitz (1988).

[86]See Rey and Stiglitz (1988), p. 4.

[87]See Rey and Stiglitz (1988), p. 13 f.

vertically integrated. In resale price maintenance (RPM) agreements, a wholesaler legally binds its customers (a number of retailers) to sell a product for not less than a specific price. RPM policies are the most frequent form of vertical restraints and are most controversially discussed.[88]

2.3.6 *Additional Market Effects*

According to economic theory, there are other market effects which can take place as a result of vertical integration. Vertically integrated enterprises have advantages when it comes to negotiation power, especially in case of scarce resources.[89] This would strengthen their market and might give them an additional edge over their (fringe and independent) competitors.

Beard, Kaserman and Mayo (2001) also discuss the possibility of the vertically integrated enterprise to sabotage the market by evading regulation. The conclusion they come up with is to have effective competition in the upstream market in order to avoid sabotage on the downstream level.[90]

References

Acemoglu D, Johnson S (2005) Unbundling institutions. J Polit Econ 113(5):949–995

Acharya V, Philippon T, Richardson M, Roubini N (2009) The financial crisis of 2007–2009: causes and remedies. Finan Markets Institutions Instrum 18(2):89–137

Altwicker T (2011) Menschenrechtlicher Gleichheitsschutz. Springer, Heidelberg

Anderson RM (1992) The core in perfectly competitive economies. In: Aumann H (ed) Handbook of game theory, Chapter 14. Elsevier Science Publishers, Amsterdam

Aumann RJ (1964) Markets with a continuum of traders. Econometrica 32(1–2):39–50

Averch H, Johnson LL (1962) Behavior of the firm under regulatory constraint. Am Econ Rev 52 (5):1052–1069

Badura P (2003) Das Berufsrecht in der Rechtsprechung des Bundesverwaltungsgerichts. In: Schmidt-Aßmann E, Sellner D, Hirsch G, Kemper GH, Lehmann-Grube H (eds) Festgabe 50 Jahre Bundesverwaltungsgericht. Carl Heymanns, Cologne, pp 785–800

Bailey EE, Coleman RD (1971) The effect of lagged regulation in an Averch-Johnson model. Bell J Econ Manage Sci 2(1):278–292

Basedow J (2004) Wirtschaftsregulierung zwischen Beschränkung und Förderung des Wettbewerbs. In: Fuchs A, Schwintowski H-P, Zimmer D (eds) Wirtschafts- und Privatrecht im Spannungsfeld von Privatautonomie. Wettbewerb und Regulierung: Festschrift für Ulrich Immenga zum 70. Geburtstag. C. H. Beck, Munich, pp 3–20

Battis U, Kersten J (2003) Die rechtlichen Rahmenbedingungen für die verhandelnde Verwaltung im Hochschulbereich. Deutsches Verwaltungsblatt 118:349–357

[88]See Deneckere et al. (1996), pp. 885–913; Shaffer (1991), pp. 120–135.

[89]See Hart and Tirole (1990), pp. 231 f.

[90]See Beard et al. (2001), pp. 319–333.

Baumol WJ, Panzar JC, Willig RD (1983) Contestable markets: an uprising in the theory of industry structure: reply. Am Econ Rev 73(3):491–496
Beard TR, Kaserman DL, Mayo JW (2001) Regulation, vertical integration and sabotage. J Ind Econ 49(3):319–333
Behrendt S, Köplin D, Kreibich R, Rogall H, Seidemann T (1996) Logistikkonzepte zur Rücknahme und Verwertung von Fernsehgeräten. In: Behrendt S, Köplin D, Kreibich R, Rogall H, Seidemann T (eds) Umweltgerechte Produktgestaltung: ECO-Design in der elektronischen Industrie. Springer, Heidelberg, pp 114–115
Benz A (1997) Privatisierung und Regulierung im Rundfunk. In: König B (ed) Privatisierung und staatliche Regulierung: Bahn, Post und Telekommunikation, Rundfunk. Nomos, Baden-Baden, pp 419–537
Bergman MA (2001) The role of the essential facilities doctrine. Antitrust Bull 46(2):403–434
Berninghaus SK, Ehrhart K-M, Güth W (2010) Strategische Spiele: eine Einführung in die Spieltheorie, 3rd edn. Springer, Berlin
Besche B (2004) Wasser und Wettbewerb: Möglichkeiten und Grenzen einer Öffnung des Wassermarkts. Peter Lang, Berlin
Boysen S, Bühring F, Franzius C, Herbst T, Kötter M, Kreutz A, von Lewinski K, Meinel F, Nolte J, Schönrock S (2007) Netzwerke: 47. Assistententagung Öffentliches Recht Berlin 2007. Tagung der Wissenschaftlichen Mitarbeiterinnen und Mitarbeiter, Wissenschaftlichen Assistentinnen und Assistenten. Nomos, Baden-Baden
Braeutigam RR, Panzar JC (1993) Effects of the change from rate-of-return to price-cap regulation. Am Econ Rev 83(2):191–198
Brunekreeft G (2003) Regulation and competition policy in the electricity market: economic analysis and german experience. Nomos, Baden-Baden
Cabral LMB, Riordan MH (1989) Incentives for cost reduction under price cap regulation. J Regul Econ 1(2):93–102
Carlton DW (2008) Should "Price Squeeze" be a recognized form of anticompetitive conduct? J Competition Law Econ 4(2):271–278
Cave ME (2007) Six degrees of separation operational separation as a remedy in european telecommunications regulation. Commun Strat 64:89–103
Cave M, Martin I (1994) The costs and benefits of accounting separation: the Australian and British debates. Telecommun Policy 18(1):12–20
Claessens S, Yurtoglu BB (2013) Corporate governance in emerging markets: a survey. Emerg Mark Rev 15:1–33
Cowan S (2002) Price-cap regulation. Swed Econ Policy Rev 9:167–188
Crew MA, Kleindorfer PR (1996) Incentive regulation in the United Kingdom and the United States: some lessons. J Regul Econ 9(3):211–225
Dehmel F (2011) Anreizregulierung von Stromübertragungsnetzen: eine Systemanalyse in Bezug auf ausgewählte Renditeeffekte. Dissertation. Katholische Universität Eichstätt-Ingolstadt, Eichstädt-Ingolstadt
Deneckere R, Marvel HP, Peck J (1996) Demand uncertainty, inventories, and resale price maintenance. Quart J Econ 111(3):885–913
Denkhaus W (2004) Die neue Institutionenökonomik und das Governancekonzept: Zum Wandel der ökonomischen Theorie und ihren Implikationen für die Verwaltungsrechtswissenschaft. In: Bungenberg M, Danz S, Heinrich H, Hünemörder O, Schmidt C, Schroeder R, Sichert A, Unroth F (eds) Recht und Ökonomik: 44. Assistententagung Öffentliches Recht Jena 2004. C. H. Beck, Munich, pp 33–60
Devlin A (2007) A proposed solution to the problem of parallel pricing in oligopolistic markets. Stanford Law Rev 59(4):1111–1151
Doidge C, Karolyi GA, Stulz RM (2007) Why do countries matter so much for corporate governance. J Financ Econ 86(1):1–39
Ebert U (1991/1992) Pigouvian tax and market structure: the case of oligopoly and different abatement technologies. FinanzArchiv/Public Finan Anal 49(2):154–166
Edwards CD (1953) Vertical integration and the monopoly problem. J Mark 17(4):404–410

Égert B (2009) Infrastructure investment in network industries: the role of incentive regulation and regulatory independence. CESifo Working paper series no. 2642
Eifert M (2006) Regulierungsstrategien. In: Hoffmann-Riem W, Schmidt-Aßmann E, Voßkuhle A (eds) Grundlagen des Verwaltungsrechts. C. H. Beck, Munich, § 19
Elsenbast W (1999) Universaldienst unter Wettbewerb: Ökonomische Analyse neuer regulierungspolitischer Ansätze zur Sicherstellung der postalischen Infrastruktur. Nomos, Baden-Baden
Endres A (1994) Strategien der Internalisierung externen Effekte: Pigou-Steuer und Coase-Theorem. FernUniversität Hagen, Hagen
Engel C, Morlok M (1998) Öffentliches Recht als ein Gegenstand ökonomischer Forschung: Die Begegnung der deutschen Staatsrechtlehre mit der Konstitutionellen Politischen Ökonomie. Mohr Siebeck, Tübingen
Eskeland GS (1994) A presumptive pigovian tax: complementing regulation to mimic an emission fee. World Bank Econ Rev 8(1):373–394
Federal German Administrative Court (2001) Entbündelter Zugang zu Teilnehmerausschlussleitungen. Neue Zeitschrift für Verwaltungsrecht 20(12):1399–1407
Follak K-P (1986) Kreditwesenaufsicht: Funktionssicherung durch Risikomanagement. Österreichische Zeitschrift für Wirtschaftsrecht 13
Foros O, Stehen F (2013) Vertical control and price cycles in gasoline retailing. Scand J Econ 115 (3):640–661
Forster F (2007) Privatisierung Regulierung der Wasserversorgung in Deutschland und den Vereinigten Staaten von Amerika. Duncker & Humblodt, Berlin
Fritsch M (2011) Marktversagen und Wirtschaftspolitik: Mikroökonomische Grundlagen staatlichen Handelns, 8th edn. Franz Vahlen, Munich
Furubotn EG, Richter R (2010) Neue Institutionenökonomik: Eine Einführung und kritische Würdigung, 4th edn. Mohr Siebeck, Tübingen
Gabrisch C (1996) Universaldienst in Deutschland: Neukonzeption für einen liberalisierten Telekommunikationsmarkt. Deutscher Universitätsverlag, Wiesbaden
Gärditz KF (2005) EG-Wettbewerbsrecht und Postmarktliberalisierung. Europäisches Wirtschafts- und Steuerrecht 2005(11):490–497
Gaudin G, Saavedra C (2014) Ex ante margin squeeze test in the telecommunications industry: what is a reasonably efficient operation. Telecommun Policy 38(2):157–172
Geradin D, O'Donoghue R (2005) The concurrent application of competition law and regulation: the case of margin squeeze abuses in the telecommunications sector. J Competition Law Econ 1(2):355–425
Ginsburg T (2005) International substitutes for domestic institutions: bilateral investment treaties and governance. Int Rev Law Econ 25(1):107–123
Granados N, Gupta A, Kauffman RJ (2010) Information transparency in business-to-consumer markets: concepts, framework, and research agenda. Inf Syst Res 21(2):207–226
Gugler K, Liebensteiner M, Schmitt S (2017) Vertical disintegration in the European electricity sector: empirical evidence on lost synergies. Int J Ind Organ 52:450–478
Hart O, Tirole J (1990) Vertical integration and market foreclosure. Brookings papers: microeconomics special issue, pp 205–286
Hayek FA (1969) Freiburger Studien: gesammelte Aufsätze. Mohr, Tübingen
Healy PM, Palepu KG (2001) Information asymmetry, corporate disclosure, and the capital markets: a review of the empirical disclosure literature. J Account Econ 31(1–3):405–440
Heimler A (2010) Is a margin squeeze an antitrust or regulatory violation. J Competition Law Econ 6(4):879–890
Holler MJ, Illing G (2009) Einführung in die Spieltheorie, 7th edn. Springer, Berlin
Holznagel B, Dörr D, Hildebrand D (2008) Elektronische Medien: Entwicklung und Regulierungsbedarf. Vahlen, Munich
Homann K, Suchanek A (2005) Ökonomik: Eine Einführung, 2nd edn. Mohr Siebeck, Tübingen
Hornby AS, Turnbull J (2010) Oxford advanced learner's dictionary of current English, 8th edn. Oxford University Press, Oxford

Hou L (2014) The abusive nature of price squeezes in the EU. Int Rev Intellect Property Competition 45:43–74
Hufen F (1994) Berufsfreiheit: Erinnerung an ein Grundrecht. Neue Juristische Wochenschrift 45:2913–2921
Hurwicz L (1995) What is the coase theorem. Jpn World Econ 7(1):49–74
Jamasb T, Pollitt M (2005) Electricity market reform in the European Union: review of progress toward liberalization & integration. Energy J 26 (Special Issue):11–41 (European Electricity Liberalisation)
Jung D (2017) Art. 102 AEUV. In: Grabitz E, Hilf M, Nettesheim M (eds) Das Recht der Europäischen Union. C.H. Beck, Munich
Kahneman D, Knetsch JL, Thaler RH (1990) Experimental tests of the endowment effect and coase theorem. J Polit Econ 98(6):1325–1348
Kamps K (2006) Rundfunkaufsicht: Ordnungsstrukturen im digitalen Zeitalter. In: Klumpp D, Kubicek H, Roßnagel A, Schulz W (eds) Medien, Ordnung und Information. Springer, Berlin, pp 133–142
Kezsbom A, Goldman AV (1996) No shortcut to antitrust analysis: the twisted journey of the "Essential Facilities" doctrine. Columbia Bus Law Rev 1996(1):1–36
Kim K, Nora V (2018) Does vertical integration enhance non-price efficiency: evidence from the movie theater industry. Working paper series economics. Nazarbayev University, Astana
Kingreen T (2005) Ein neuer rechtlicher Rahmen für einen Binnenmarkt für Gesundheitsleistungen. Neue Zeitschrift für Sozialrecht 2005(10):505–511
Knittel CR (2006) The adoption of state electricity regulation: the role of interest groups. J Ind Econ 54(2):201–222
Kühling J (2004) Sektorspezifische Regulierung in den Netzwirtschaften. C. H. Beck, Munich
Kümpel S, Wittig A (2011) Bank- und Kapitalmarktrecht, 4th edn. Dr. Otto Schmidt, Cologne
Ladeur K-H (2005) Die Wissenschaftsfreiheit der „entfesselten Hochschule": Umgestaltung der Hochschulen nach Ermessen des Staates? Die Öffentliche Verwaltung 58(18):753–764
Lipsky AB, Sidak JG (1998) Essential facilities. Stanford Law Rev 51(5):1187–1248
Liston C (1993) Price-cap versus rate-of-return regulation. J Regul Econ 5(1):25–48
Lyon TP (1996) A model of sliding-scale regulation. J Regul Econ 9(3):227–247
Maskin E, Tirole J (1988) A theory of dynamic oligopoly, II: price competition, kinked demand curves, and edgeworth cycles. Econometrica 56(3):571–599
Möllinger C (2009) Eigentumsrechtliche Entflechtung der Übertragungsnetze: Unter besonderer Berücksichtigung des 3. Binnenmarktpaketes für Energie. Peter Lang, Bern
Montoya MA, Trillas F (2009) The measurement of regulator independence in practice: Latin America and the Caribbean. Int J Public Policy 4(1–2):113–134
Nicolaides P (1992) Competition among rules. World Competition 16(2):113–121
Niemeier H-M (2002) Regulation of airports: the case of Hamburg airport—a view from the perspective of regional policy. J Air Transport Manage 8(1):37–48
Nocke V, Rey P (2018) Exclusive dealing and vertical integration in interlocking relationships. J Econ Theory 177:183–221
Noel MD (2016) Pricing strategies and litigation risks: an economic analysis of the downstream petroleum industry. J Competition Law Econ 12(2):287–311
Normann H-T (2008) Vertical integration, raising rivals' costs and upstream collusion. Preprints of the Max Planck Institute for Research on Collective Goods. Max Planck Institute for Research on Collective Goods 2008/30, Bonn
Pareto V (1906) Manuale di economia politica. Facsimile of the first edition published in Milan. Schäffer-Poeschel, Stuttgart 1992
Pint EM (1992) Price-cap versus rate-of-return regulation in a stochastic-cost model. Rand J Econ 23(4):564–578
Pollitt M (2008) The arguments for and against ownership unbundling of energy transmission networks. Energy Policy 36(2):704–713

Pünder H (2006) Zertifizierung und Akkreditierung: private Qualitätskontrolle unter staatlicher Gewährleistungsverantwortung. Zeitschrift für das gesamte Handelsrecht und Wirtschaftsrecht 170:567–599
Rey P, Stiglitz J (1988) Vertical restraints and producers' competition. NBER working paper series no. 2601. National Bureau of Economic Research, Cambridge
Rieck C (2007) Spieltheorie: eine Einführung, 7th edn. Rieck, Eschborn
Riedel D (2012) Eigentum, Enteignung und das Wohl der Allgemeinheit: Zur Ausgestaltungsgarantie der Eigentumsgewährleistung, zum Enteignungsbegriff und zur Gemeinwohlbindung der Enteignung. Duncker & Humblot, Berlin
Riordan MH (1998) Anticompetitive vertical integration by a dominant firm. Am Econ Rev 88 (5):1232–1248
Riordan MH, Salop SC (1995) Evaluating vertical mergers—a post Chicago approach. Antitrust Law J 63(2):513–568
Robinson J (1934) What is perfect competition? Q J Econ 49(1):104–120
Rockholz A (2001) Organisationsformen in der privaten Abfallwirtschaft. Zeitschrift für Umwelt- und Technikrecht 56
Rutkowsky S (1998) Abfallpolitik in der Kreislaufwirtschaft. Erich Schmidt, Berlin
Säcker FJ (2009) Die wettbewerbsorientierte Anreizregulierung von Netzwirtschaften. Netzwirtschaften & Recht 6(2):78–85
Salinger MA (1988) Vertical mergers and market foreclosure. Q J Econ 103(2):345–356
Schmalensee R (1989) Good regulatory regimes. Rand J Econ 20(3):417–436
Schmidt-Assmann E (1993) Die Wissenschaftsfreiheit nach Art. 5 Abs. 3 GG als Organisationsgrundsatz. In: Bull HP, Seewald O, Becker B (eds.) Festschrift Thieme: Zum 70. Geburtstag. Carl Heymanns, Cologne, pp 697–711
Scholtka B (2005) Das neue Energiewirtschaftsgesetz. Neue Juristische Wochenschrift 2005 (34):2421–2425
Semigran HL, Gourevitch R, Sinaiko AD, Cowling D, Mehrotra A (2017) Patients' views on price shopping and price transparency. Am J Managed Care 23(6):E186–E192
Shaffer G (1991) Slotting allowances and resale price maintenance: a comparison of facilitating practices. RAND J Econ 22(1):120–135
Sherman R (1977) Financial aspects of rate-of-return regulation. South Econ J 44(2):240–248
Sidak JG (2008) Abolishing the price squeeze as a theory of antitrust liability. J Competition Law Econ 4(2):279–309
Siegwarth Meyer C, Wang Y (2011) Determining the competitive effects of vertical integration in mergers. Econ Committee Newsl 11(1):7–11
Smith W (1997) Utility regulators: the independence debate, public policy for the private sector. Note no. 127. World Bank Group
Solomon E (1970) Alternative rate of return concepts and their implications for utility regulation. Bell J Econ Manage Sci 1(1):65–81
Soma JT, Forkner DA, Jumps BP (1998) The essential facilities doctrine in the deregulated telecommunications industry. Berkeley Technol Law J 13(2):565–614
Spann RM (1974) Rate of return regulation and efficiency in production: an empirical test of the Averch-Johnson thesis. Bell J Econ Manage Sci 5(1):38–52
Spengler JJ (1950) Vertical integration and antitrust policy. J Polit Econ 58(4):347–352
Stahler F, Upmann T (2008) Market entry regulation and international competition. Rev Int Econ 16(4):611–626
Steiner F (2000) Regulation, industry structure, and performance in the electricity supply industry. OECD working papers. ECO/WKP(2000)11. OECD, Paris
Stern J (1997) What makes an independent regulator independent? Lond Bus Sch Rev 8(2):67–74
Stigler GJ (1957) Perfect competition, historically contemplated. J Polit Econ 65(1):1–17
Storr S (2006) Soll das Recht der Regulierungsverwaltung übergreifend geregelt werden? Deutsches Verwaltungsblatt 121(16):1017–1026
Taggart RA (1981) Rate-of-return regulation and utility capital structure decisions. J Finance 36 (2):383–393

van Aken A (2004) Vom Nutzen der ökonomischen Theorie für das öffentliche Recht: Methode und Anwendungsmöglichkeiten. In: Bungenberg M, Danz S, Heinrich H, Hünemörder O, Schmidt C, Schroeder R, Sichert A, Unroth F (eds) Recht und Ökonomik: 44. Assistententagung Öffentliches Recht Jena 2004. C. H. Beck, Munich, pp 1–32

Voßkuhle A (2003) Beteiligung Privater an der Wahrnehmung öffentlicher Aufgaben und staatlicher Verantwortung. Veröffentlichungen der Vereinigung Deutscher Staatsrechtslehrer (VVDStRL) 62:266–335

Watson R (1998) EU attempts to tackle parallel pricing of drugs. BMJ 316(7147):1769

Wieland J (1995) Der Wandel von Verwaltungsaufgaben als Folge der Postprivatisierung. Die Verwaltung 28(3):315–335

Wollenschläger F (2013) Effektiver Rechtsschutz bei informationellen Maßnahmen der öffentlichen Hand am Beispiel der novellierten Informationsbefugnis im Lebensmittelrecht (§ 40 LFGB). Die Öffentliche Verwaltung 1:7–16

Yamawake T, Yamoto S, Goi HC, Lee D-J (2018) Determinants of vertical integration: investment efficiency, product differentiation and firm size. Theor Econ Lett 8:1028–1043

Chapter 3
Evaluation of Vertical Integration

A number of theorists have dealt with the effects of vertical integration as well as the thread of vertical foreclosure as an important effect of vertical integration. Riordan (1998) identifies the possibility of preventing market entry after vertical integration and the availability of superior technology for the integrated enterprise as crucial factors to determine the effects of vertical integration.[1] The economic and legal aspects of regulation in general and vertical integration in particular are the framework for the assessment.

Riordan and Salop[2] (1995) developed a model to evaluate and assess the effect vertical integration has on competition. In the following section, the general concerns and positive aspects concerning vertical integration (Sect. 3.1) are presented. In contrast, the negative aspects of vertical integration are also assessed in the following sections. The key element of the negative effects in this model is the (potential) for market foreclosure. That is why two possible ways of market foreclosure will be investigated, namely the foreclosure of inputs (Sect. 3.2) and the foreclosure of customers (Sect. 3.3). Other possible negative effects (Sect. 3.4) are presented. Positive and negative effects are weighed against each other in a final step (Sect. 3.5). The model is based on these legal and economic aspects. Based on the findings of the model, theses for possible amendments of the regulation of vertical integration are drawn.

[1]See Riordan (1998), p. 1246; for additional theories on vertical integration see Chap. 2.
[2]See Riordan and Salop (1995), pp. 513–568; there are other approaches which are less comprehensive, but that do not add any additional aspects to it, these approaches can be found in Salinger (1988), pp. 345–356; Siegwarth Meyer and Wang (2011), pp. 7–11; Normann (2008); Foros and Stehen (2013), pp. 640–661; Rey and Stiglitz (1988); Hart and Tirole (1990), pp. 205–286; Beard et al. (2001), pp. 319–333.

C. Kleineberg, *Vertical Integration and Regulation*, SpringerBriefs in Law,
https://doi.org/10.1007/978-3-030-11358-2_3

3.1 General Concerns and Positive Aspects

On the one hand, there are a number of negative aspects that are expected after vertical integration. The general concerns regarding vertical integration are the incentive to increase the costs of doing business for competitors. The most extreme way of doing so is through foreclosures (see Sects. 3.2 and 3.3). Additionally, vertical integration may facilitate coordinated conduct due to a reduced number of enterprises in a market. Moreover, the vertically integrated enterprise might intend to increase the costs of its competitors. Consequently, they could have an advantage in market levels at which they are competing against non-vertically integrated enterprises.

On the other hand, there are several positive aspects of vertical integration. These effects are predominantly efficiency effects. Vertical integration can facilitate coordination when it comes to product design. A coordinated product design would also lower production costs and might lead to a higher product quality as well as shorter lead times. Also, promotion costs could be reduced, because free riders would be unable to profit from intensive marketing with a similar product. An enterprise that would profit from increased numbers in sales on multiple levels would increase its promotion and marketing benefits. As a result of that, enterprises would not just market their products and services so that retailers want to sell it (push marketing), but also market directly to final customers so that they enter stores and ask for a particular product or service (pull marketing).[3]

Another efficiency gain which is given in the model is the elimination of a double mark-up which is also frequently referred to as eliminating double marginalization. If both markets are working imperfectly, a monopoly profit might be achieved on the wholesale and the retail level. This would be avoided by having a vertically integrated enterprise which would only reap the monopoly profit once.[4] Economic theory can show and provide proof of the efficiency gains which result from this.[5]

The pivotal challenge for competition authorities is to balance the efficiency gains and the efficiency losses of vertical integration. Unlike the traditional Chicago-School-approach, Riordan and Salop (1995) relax the assumption of the single monopoly theory. It is no longer assumed that there is a monopoly supplier in the case of vertical integration.[6]

[3]See Riordan and Salop (1995), pp. 523 ff.

[4]See Riordan and Salop (1995), p. 526.

[5]For further information on the effect of the elimination of double marginalization see Durham (2000), pp. 207–229; Gaudet and Van Long (1996); Lantz (2009), pp. 434–439.

[6]See Riordan and Salop (1995), p. 517.

3.2 Foreclosure of Inputs

A vertically integrated enterprise may exclude downstream competitors from access to important inputs or increase the prices for them. Consequently, their own downstream operations would have a cost advantage. When refraining from the idea of perfect competition and acknowledging shortcomings and pitfalls of the market, other input suppliers might not be able to compensate and supply other non-vertically-integrated downstream enterprises. Furthermore, their market power could be increased and they would be in a position to charge a higher price. In addition, vertical integration of one enterprise might facilitate collusion under other input suppliers.[7]

This behaviour could result in a deadweight loss and a welfare loss primarily for consumers. As a result, vertical integration contains a risk of price increases and welfare losses for consumers based on input foreclosure. Whether or not enterprises use this means, depends on a number of different economic factors.[8]

When considering anti-competitive harm, the model conducts a four step analysis. Firstly, the possible impact on input prices is calculated. The question is whether or not other input suppliers would join the market if prices increased. If there are a broad variety of substitute inputs, rivals might not be harmed. This step additionally assesses the competition on the foreclosed market. In the case of significant competition in the market with equally cost-efficient competitors, an input foreclosure or a cost increase for inputs is impossible. Furthermore, enterprises would not follow the integrated enterprise's cost increase, if there was strong competition in a market. Another consideration is the question of which interests the vertically integrated enterprise has in competition. If an enterprise has more to gain from expanding its sales of input goods and/or services than its competitors, it is very unlikely to foreclose downstream enterprises from inputs or to increase the input prices.[9]

The elasticity of the input demand also has to be determined. In the case of high price elasticity of demand, price increases seldom take place. In addition, the likelihood of price discrimination has to be estimated. The final question about the impact on input prices is whether or not a disruptive price setting competitor is integrated. If a previously vertically integrated enterprise put its competitors under pressure by lowering prices, it's acquisition or integration into a larger enterprise would increase the likelihood of price increases by other enterprises. This occurs because these other enterprises are no longer under pressure of having their prices undercut by these particular enterprises.[10]

The second step is the assessment of the anticompetitive effect in the output market. This does not solely focus on the wholesale market, but rather on the downstream market. It investigates whether or not there are substitute products

---

[7] See Riordan and Salop (1995), p. 528.

[8] See Riordan and Salop (1995), p. 529.

[9] See Riordan and Salop (1995), pp. 533 f.

[10] See Riordan and Salop (1995), pp. 536 ff.

available which consumers could buy instead of the products offered by vertically integrated enterprises, if they increased in price.[11] Another part of the assessment is the degree of competition in the downstream market. If the prices of an input factor for rival enterprises increase, there is an expected decrease of competition with one enterprise having a competitive edge. Nevertheless, vertically integrated enterprises with a strong substitute product might not be affected by this price increase and would be able to supply consumers at a lower price. In this case, there would be no incentive for a price increase by the vertically integrated enterprise. The relevant factors for this investigation also include the ease of entry for new competitors and the likelihood of other downstream operators to increase their prices for consumers.[12]

Furthermore it is necessary to consider the impact foreclosure on the upstream market has on the profits of the vertically integrated enterprise. These profits depend on the magnitude of the price increase that are accepted by the consumers, the pre-integration share of the downstream division, the expansion of output that is expected and the profit margin of the vertically integrated enterprise. If many other enterprises profit significantly from an increase in market prices as a result of a price increase by the vertically integrated enterprise, the vertically integrated enterprise is likely to refrain from doing it.[13]

Additionally, whether or not the enterprise on the downstream level which was vertically integrated had the role of a "maverick" competitor on the downstream market is important. In this role, the enterprise was undercutting its rivals' costs and therefore putting them under constant pressure to maintain low prices. If such an enterprise is integrated vertically, it will stop undercutting the prices of competitors and will likely engage in price coordination with its downstream rivals. In return, this would facilitate the coordination of prices on the upstream level from which the enterprise as a whole profits.[14]

Furthermore, it is important to assess the degree of product differentiation on the downstream market. In the case of a very homogenous product and collaborative conduct by enterprises on the market, it is very difficult for consumers to switch to another product after a price increase. In the case of highly differentiated products, it is easier and therefore more likely that customers will switch.[15] Another factor is the magnitude of the increase in rivals' cost. This also takes the cost impact of an individual input factor on the downstream price into consideration. If machinery enterprises purchase enterprises that supply them with instruction labels, a price increase in those labels will not have a significant impact on the price increase of the final machine.[16] Finally, it is worth considering whether or not the increase in

[11]See Riordan and Salop (1995), p. 539.

[12]See Riordan and Salop (1995), pp. 539 f.

[13]See Riordan and Salop (1995), p. 541.

[14]See Riordan and Salop (1995), p. 542.

[15]See Riordan and Salop (1995), pp. 542 f.

[16]See Riordan and Salop (1995), pp. 543 ff.

input costs takes place at a variable or fixed level. That means that the cost increase might occur for a good or service that is not necessary upon producing more goods or providing more services. An example of this would be the purchase of a machine or the certification and accreditation of processes.[17]

The third step is to assess the effects of input foreclosure on related markets. According to Riordan and Salop's (1995) definition of "related markets", the term refers to substitute products and services which consumers might consider. Up until now, substitution has been considered an activity which takes place in the upstream or the downstream market. In this stage, the focus is on customers and also deals with complementary goods and services.[18]

As a fourth step, the net competitive effect is evaluated based on the findings from previous steps.[19] The first step assesses the potential harm to enterprises in the upstream market. The second and third steps assess the harm which could occur to consumers. All steps deal with the effects and the likelihood of input foreclosure. In order to show the negative effects, a necessary condition is to indicate a price increase which could take place on the upstream level. If a price increase takes place on the upstream level, it would harm competitors. A price increase could also take place on the downstream level and harm consumers. Nevertheless, when attempting to show the harm inflicted on consumers there are various shortcomings to take into consideration. These shortcomings arise especially because consumers might have long-term contracts which do not indicate price effects immediately.[20]

3.3 Foreclosure of Costumers

The second dimension in which negative effects may occur is the foreclosure of customers. Customer foreclosure refers to a scenario in which a vertically integrated enterprise no longer buys products and services from other enterprises on the upstream market. Consequently, the non-integrated enterprise might no longer have a viable customer base or might no longer be able to profit from economies of scale and therefore be unable to provide sufficiently low prices. As a result of these factors, the non-integrated enterprise would have to leave the market.[21]

There are four steps to assess the likelihood of foreclosure of consumers. Beyond these four steps, the magnitude of the expected effects should also be investigated. The first step is to assess the impact on rivals' costs and viability. The underlying idea is to investigate whether or not there are other customers available in the upstream market. Additionally, it is necessary to define the minimum viable scale

[17]See Riordan and Salop (1995), p. 545.

[18]See Riordan and Salop (1995), p. 546 f.

[19]See Riordan and Salop (1995), p. 547.

[20]See Riordan and Salop (1995), pp. 549 f.

[21]See Riordan and Salop (1995), pp. 551 f.

for an enterprise in the upstream level. If the viable scale is very high and/or the vertically integrated enterprise previously bought a significant share of the (now) upstream competitor's products and services, the vertically non-integrated enterprise is very likely to exit the market as a result of integration.[22] Even if the independent competitor manages to remain in the market, there might be a negative effect on marginal costs as a result of the foreclosure in the upstream market by the vertically integrated enterprise. Additionally, one needs to consider the effect the reduced customer base has for enterprises in the upstream market to invest in cost reduction efforts. Given a smaller customer base and consequently a lower output, some investments take significantly longer to amortise.[23]

The second step is the evaluation of the impact in the ancillary markets. Ancillary markets are markets that use the same input, but do not produce the same output like the vertically-integrated enterprise. If an input supplier has to exit a market because of vertical integration, this has a negative impact on the ancillary market, because that market loses a supplier. This occurs when customers in ancillary markets are unable to substitute to alternative products due to the reduction of competition which results from input suppliers exiting the market.[24]

The third step is to assess the anticompetitive impact in the foreclosed customer market. This means that after enterprises exit the upstream market, the likelihood that remaining enterprises increase their prices or coordinate their pricing behaviour increases. This in return would have an impact on the input prices, the prices on the downstream market and the ancillary markets.[25]

3.4 Other Possible Effects

Vertical integration might have additional possible effects on competition. The most prominent effects include the exchange of information and the (potential) evasion of regulation. These effects will be outlined in this section.

Vertically integrated enterprises possess a higher likelihood to exchange anti-competitive information. Another effect is the higher likelihood of explicit or tacit collusion.

Information exchange should raise concerns when that information is unique, projectable to other business fields and levels and is able to influence pricing decisions. This information might give the vertically integrated enterprise an edge in price negotiations. Furthermore, the exchange of information might be able to facilitate collusive conduct in a market.[26]

---

[22]See Riordan and Salop (1995), p. 554.

[23]See Riordan and Salop (1995), pp. 555 f.

[24]See Riordan and Salop (1995), p. 556.

[25]See Riordan and Salop (1995), pp. 556 f.

[26]See Riordan and Salop (1995), pp. 557 ff.

Furthermore, vertically integrated enterprises may be able to evade regulation. In the case of maximum price regulations or price discrimination regulation, vertically integrated enterprises cannot be investigated without major difficulties by the competition authorities. They could easily circumvent maximum price regulation by internally shifting costs between different levels (wholesale and retail level). By doing so, they would also be able to evade price discrimination or other anti-competitive pricing patterns that have been subject to prohibition like predatory pricing or limit pricing.[27]

3.5 Assessment of Positive and Negative Aspects

In the final step, positive and negative aspects are weighed against each other with their various weights assessed.

The conclusion of this assessment does not have to answer the question of whether an enterprise should be vertically separated or not. It may also include an assessment of which legal norms might help to fix or reduce negative aspects of vertical integration while still allowing enterprises to reap efficiency gains.[28]

The model allows an ex-ante assessment of the impact of possible vertical integration. At the same time, it can be used to assess ex-post, the impact a high vertical integration has on competition in a particular market.

3.6 Preliminary Conclusion

Vertical integration is not necessarily a threat to consumer welfare. It might, however, be subject to efficiency gains and eliminate double marginalization. Nevertheless, being vertically integrated allows several options for enterprises to abuse their position. When dealing with capacity shortages, charging different prices or deciding to refuse supply to vertically non-integrated enterprises, vertical integration could lead to negative outcomes such as the elimination or reduction of competition.

Additionally, vertically integrated enterprises are difficult to regulate, because they have all the information available that regulation authorities lack. Consequently, regulation is becoming challenging.

---

[27] See Riordan and Salop (1995), pp. 561 f.

[28] See Riordan and Salop (1995), p. 564.

References

Beard TR, Kaserman DL, May JW (2001) Regulation, vertical integration and sabotage. J Ind Econ 49(3):319–333

Durham Y (2000) An experimental examination of double marginalization and vertical relationships. J Econ Behav Organ 42(2):207–229

Foros O, Stehen F (2013) Vertical control and price cycles in gasoline retailing. Scand J Econ 115 (3):640–661

Gaudet G, Van Long N (1996) Vertical integration, foreclosure, and profits in the presence of double marginalization. J Econ Manage Strategy 5:409–432

Hart O, Tirole J (1990) Vertical integration and market foreclosure. Brookings papers: microeconomics special issue, pp 205–286

Lantz B (2009) The double marginalization problem of transfer pricing: theory and experiment. Eur J Oper Res 196(2):434–439

Normann H-T (2008) Vertical integration, raising rivals' costs and upstream collusion. Preprints of the Max Planck Institute for Research on Collective Goods. Max Planck Institute for Research on Collective Goods 2008/30, Bonn

Rey P, Stiglitz J (1988) Vertical restraints and producers' competition. NBER working paper series no. 2601. National Bureau of Economic Research, Cambridge

Riordan MH (1998) Anticompetitive vertical integration by a dominant firm. Am Econ Rev 88 (5):1232–1248

Riordan MH, Salop SC (1995) Evaluating vertical mergers—a post chicago approach. Antitrust Law J 63(2):513–568

Salinger MA (1988) Vertical mergers and market foreclosure. Q J Econ 103(2):345–356

Siegwarth Meyer C, Wang Y (2011) Determining the competitive effects of vertical integration in mergers. Econ Committee Newsl 11(1):7–11

Chapter 4
Legal Implications and Suggested Amendments

In this section, various legal implications of improving competition in markets are presented based on the application of the model by Riordan and Salop. At first the existing/current legal obligation is presented. Knowledge of the existing regulatory framework allows for an assessment to be conducted. Thereafter, the legal shortcomings and suggested legal amendments are also outlined.

Theses 1–6 suggest legal amendments whilst these 7–9 outline activities and structural modifications for regulation authorities. Lastly, thesis 10 gives an outlook of major fields in which regulation is needed in the future (thesis 10). As a whole, the suggested activities represent a comprehensive set of modifications that allow for more competition in different sectors and consequently increase consumer welfare as well as aggregated welfare.

4.1 Vertically Integrated Enterprises Shall Be Obliged to Forward Their Price Development Rationale to the Federal German Cartel Office to Have It Investigated in Order to Determine Whether or not They Violate the Prohibition of Margin-Squeezes

4.1.1 Current Legal Obligations

Some markets are under special investigation by the German competition authorities. One example of this is the German gasoline sector. Under the existing legal regime, all gasoline retailers are obliged to forward information on all prices within five minutes to the gasoline market transparency unit of the Federal German Cartel Office. This entity forwards the data to consumer information services that publish the live price data on the internet or via smartphone apps.

C. Kleineberg, *Vertical Integration and Regulation*, SpringerBriefs in Law,
https://doi.org/10.1007/978-3-030-11358-2_4

In special circumstances, the Federal German Cartel Office can also request the quantities of gasoline that have been sold within a particular time. It used this tool to investigate the reasons behind the price increases of gasoline around the Easter holidays, which were strongly criticized in the German public.

An additional legal obligation is the prohibition of margin squeeze pricing. According to §20 (2) No. 3 German Act against Restraints of Competition (GWB), an enterprise with significant market power is prohibited to charge prices at the retail level that are below the prices at the wholesale level.

4.1.2 Legal Shortcomings

There is plenty of information available on gasoline prices at the retail level, but there is no information available on possible cross-subsidization of downstream operations.

Furthermore, the prohibition of margin squeeze pricing according to the German GWB contains a very weak element of offence. Applying a different definition of margin squeeze would enable competition and regulation authorities to more effectively prevent pricing patterns that intend to reduce competition by independent enterprises.

Nevertheless, there is an intense debate about whether or not margin squeeze pricing is a pattern that is used at all. It is contradictory to the idea of profit maximization to make losses in order to eliminate competitors in the hope that they would not return to the market and consequently generate the monopoly price in consecutive periods.

For example, the gasoline market cannot be considered a contestable market as there are significant barriers to entry in the retail and wholesale market due to environmental and other security regulations. Furthermore, there are high sunk costs for the equipment needed and gasoline stations can quickly adapt their prices.

4.1.3 Legal and Constitutional Restraints

An exchange or provision of information might interfere with an enterprise's protection of business secrets. Business secrets are also protected by fundamental rights of the GG, especially Art. 2 GG, Art. 12 GG and Art. 14 GG. Consequently, the data processing procedures would have to adhere to strict data protection standards. In order for the measure to be proportional, there have to be major reservations with regards to price discrimination. Additionally milder tools with the same affect of forwarding the price rationale to regulatory authorities should not exist.

4.1.4 Suggested Legal Amendment

Regulation authorities in many cases lack information needed to investigate whether or not an individual legal norm has been violated by an enterprise. As a result, enterprises shall forward their internal pricing rationale to competition authorities to have it investigated, considering all conditions with regards to business secrets and evaluated on the grounds of a competitive market.

4.2 Refusal to Supply Shall Become an Element of Offence in German Competition Law

4.2.1 Current Legal Obligation

There is no specific legislation on the refusal to supply many markets in Germany. Additionally, the traditional universal service obligation only applies if a single enterprise is in a dominant market position. This does not apply to a situation in which the dominant market position is jointly held by a group of enterprises that are highly interdependent them.

4.2.2 Legal Shortcoming

§ 21 GWB prohibits boycotting another enterprise. This element of offence is different from the refusal to supply. Boycotting refers to organising a common front against an individual enterprise. Refusal to supply is not prohibited under German competition law.

By being able to prevent independent retailers from having access to raw or semi-final products in the wholesale market the major retailers have a tool to put pressure on independent enterprises. Oligopoly situations in particular are not explicitly covered by the prohibition to abuse market dominance as this concept primarily applies to single enterprises.

Consequently, if engagement in margin squeezing is prohibited, enterprises might use the refusal to supply as a means of harming their vertically non-integrated competitors. The circumvention of regulation is easily possible.

4.2.3 Legal and Constitutional Restraints

The prohibition of the refusal to supply interferes with the freedom of property, because it dictates to enterprises whether or not they have the right to refuse to deal with another enterprise. Nevertheless, the social obligations of property ownership limit the fundamental freedoms of property. There need to be restrictions and conditions for the prohibition of the refusal to supply.

From a European perspective, the crucial aim is the protection of the European market and the enablement of competition. Consequently, there are no significant restrictions for an element of offence of "refusal to supply".

4.2.4 Suggested Legal Amendment

Refusal to supply should be added to the GWB as an element of offence, in particular to the prohibited market conduct according to §20 GWB. As a result, vertically integrated enterprises will not be able to circumvent regulation in particular market conduct that would harm vertically non-integrated enterprises such as the prohibition of margin squeeze, the prohibition of limit or predatory pricing and related patterns.

4.3 Price Discrimination on Highly Concentrated Markets Must Be Subject to Strict Regulation

4.3.1 Current Legal Obligation

According to existing competition law, especially §20 GWB, charging lower prices at the downstream level as opposed to the upstream level is prohibited. This element of offence only prohibits the most extreme form of abuse of market power. All other pricing patterns are allowed as a freedom right of the enterprise.

4.3.2 Legal Shortcoming

The existing legal provision does allow for vertically non-integrated enterprises to be placed at a significant disadvantage compared to vertically integrated enterprises. Vertically integrated enterprises could use their market power or oligopoly at a certain level of the supply chain to charge a monopoly price at that level or to put the vertically non-integrated enterprise at a significant disadvantage. This pricing disadvantage could be used to eliminate competitors that previously had been undercutting the price of the vertically integrated enterprise.

4.3.3 Legal and Constitutional Restraints

Prohibiting price discrimination would limit freedom of property and professional freedom. Consequently, the requirements for limiting freedom of property and professional freedom need to be met.

4.3.4 Suggested Legal Amendment

According to § 32e GWB German competition and regulation authorities are allowed to gain access to business information on sold quantities etc. This needs to be expanded to grant the authorities access to the materials that underline the pricing rationale and internal pricing systems of enterprises. That is how the authorities are able to monitor whether or not the enterprises are charging the same prices for vertically non-integrated enterprises as they are for themselves.

4.4 A Complaint Structure Is Needed to Detect Lacking Competition in Individual Sectors

4.4.1 Current Legal Obligation

The Federal German Cartel Office is investigating individual sectors based upon necessity which is derived from among others complaints by consumers or competitors. The underlying mechanisms and the threshold for the investigation are not explained.

4.4.2 Legal Shortcoming

With a lack of supporting documents and an explanation of which factors are causing the start of market investigations, the regulation appears to be rather arbitrary and the question of political power play and the influence of lobbyism and political populism seem to determine which sector will be investigated in greater depth.

4.4.3 Legal and Constitutional Restraints

There might be reservations regarding the criteria that are established and some due process concerns. Nevertheless, establishing and justifying a complaint structure for consumers and other enterprises does not contain significant legal and constitutional restraints.

4.4.4 *Suggested Legal Amendment*

The competition and regulation authorities need to define a transparent set of rules and criteria which can be easily operationalized to determine which sectors should be investigated in detail.

4.5 There Needs to Be a Regulation on How to Deal with Capacity Shortages

4.5.1 *Current Legal Obligation*

There is no regulation on how to deal with capacity shortages in the light of vertically integrated and non-integrated enterprises. In the case of capacity shortages, the supply for competing enterprises could simply be halted and enterprises would subsequently have to stop their operations.

4.5.2 *Legal Shortcoming*

Under the given regulation, vertically non-integrated enterprises will suffer in the case of capacity shortages, because the vertically integrated enterprise will always supply its own downstream operations first. In the end they would be unable to remain in the market due to the losses they made in the period of the capacity shortage.

4.5.3 *Legal and Constitutional Restraints*

Regulating capacity shortages interferes with the freedom of property of an enterprise. This is protected by Art. 14 GG. Furthermore, it is be possible to compare the regulation of capacity shortages with the temporary substitution of a market system with a centralized planned economy. As a result, there need to by high burdens for the regulation of capacity shortages. This regulation must be perceived as a response to market failure and seen as a temporary intervention rather than a medium or long-term interference.

4.5.4 Suggested Legal Amendment

There needs to be a regulation on how to deal with capacity shortages that occur in markets with dominant enterprises. The underlying rationale has to be that in case of capacity shortages in markets with a high concentration, scarce resources have to be supplied to vertically integrated as well as vertically non-integrated enterprises according to the market share prior to the capacity shortage or some other measure of equivalent effect and logic.

4.6 A Vertical Separation Is the Ultima Rationale and Shall Be Introduced to Competition and Regulation Law

4.6.1 Current Legal Obligation

The market structure of particular markets has its flaws, but these can be fixed based on the above mentioned legal modifications. Consequently, a vertical separation of the sector is not to be considered necessary in the cases that have been investigated by the Federal German Cartel Office thus far. Furthermore, double marginalization and numerous efficiency gains can be secured by maintaining the vertically integrated market structure. The potential threats should be addressed and diminished. Legally there is no regulation which allows vertical separation as a tool in competition and regulation law.

4.6.2 Legal Shortcoming

Despite the high market power of the five major enterprises in the German gasoline markets, there are means to stimulate and protect competition beyond vertical separation and unbundling.

Nevertheless, the possibility of vertically separating an enterprise should become an option for competition and regulation authorities. Given the significance of vertical separation, however, its use must still be subject to very strict conditions.

4.6.3 Legal and Constitutional Restraints

There is no unbundling tool as an element for regulation law. Even if there was an unbundling tool in regulation law, there would be severe boundaries for its use as laid by fundamental freedoms.

Forcing an enterprise to unbundle has a major interference with the freedom of property and can be seen as a means of expropriation. Although the protective level of fundamental and constitutional freedoms and rights is not very high, it represents an important barrier.

4.6.4 *Suggested Legal Amendment*

Although vertical separation is not necessary, it should be introduced as a means of regulation law. In doing so, there need to be clear guidelines on how and when to use this tool. The two main conditions are that vertical separation or unbundling has to be the last resort and that a major infringement which has led to a substantial loss in consumer welfare (and societal welfare as a whole) has taken place.

4.7 Consumers Need to Be Educated on How the Market Functions in Order to Inform Them About Oligopoly Collusion Tactics of Major Enterprises in Particular Markets

4.7.1 *Current Legal Obligation*

The creation of a gasoline market transparency unit and the public access of gasoline prices was a positive effort to investigate the functioning of a market. This unit conducts comprehensive examinations of how individual markets function. The findings are published in papers on a regular basis.

4.7.2 *Legal Shortcoming*

Although market transparency can be used as a reasonable tool for consumers to be aware of pricing patterns of enterprises and can assist consumers in buying a homogenous good for the lowest price, this system has significant shortcomings. While consumers are aware of the market prices, enterprises can themselves monitor the market at significantly lower costs. In highly concentrated oligopoly markets this can facilitate collusion.

Additionally, the reports and publications of the Federal German Cartel Office do not target a broad audience of consumers. They do contain a variety of graphs that explain pricing patterns, but the take-away for consumers are not easily phrased. These recommendations are still an important first step of the Federal German Cartel Office to educate consumers about the functioning of particular markets.

4.7.3 Legal and Constitutional Restraints

In the case of the gasoline sector and educating consumers about market mechanisms, there are no legal or constitutional restraints that limit the public administration in their task to educate consumers.

4.7.4 Suggested Legal Amendment

Possible legal amendments would be a shift of resources from simply monitoring the market to educating consumers directly or indirectly with publications about market mechanisms. They also need to be more easily approachable and far more comprehensible than the reports that were recently published by the German Federal Cartel Office on the observations in the gasoline markets.

These pricing patterns shall be investigated in other markets as well. Additionally, advice needs to be given to consumers on when, where and how to find the lowest price in order to stimulate competition among enterprises.

4.8 The German Competition Authorities Should Continue Monitoring Mergers in Highly Concentrated Markets

4.8.1 Current Legal Obligation

In the past, the Federal German Cartel Office has prohibited acquisitions of independent gasoline retailers. It is necessary to continue doing so in order to keep disruptive pricing enterprises in the market. Otherwise they could be pushed out of the market. According to § 32e GWB it is possible to start investigations concerning the competitiveness of markets.

4.8.2 Legal Shortcoming

There are no detailed criteria for the investigation of economic sectors. Once a consumer or enterprise complains to the Federal German Cartel Office in a non-standardized process and these complaints reach a certain unclear and undefined threshold, the Federal German Cartel Office starts its investigation.

4.8.3 Legal and Constitutional Restraints

The investigation would be conducted on the legal grounds of existing norms. The freedom of equity and professional freedom possibly interfere with activities of the state. Nevertheless, they can be limited by law.

4.8.4 Suggested Legal Amendment

This point outlines primarily the fact that regulation authorities should continue their activities.

4.9 German Regulation Authorities Should Investigate the Efficiency of the Level of the Upstream Market of Highly Concentrated Industries

The high concentration and joined ownership of refinery capacity in Germany could facilitate collusion in the upstream market of the gasoline industry. With high market entry barriers the sector as well as many other sectors might experience a significant threat of reduced or lacking competitiveness.

4.9.1 Current Legal Obligation

Currently, the obligation to forward information on the costs and return to investment of operating refineries can be used by competition and regulation authorities according to § 59 GWB. Nevertheless, this tool is seldom used.

4.9.2 Legal Shortcomings

The structure of the upstream market of the German retail gasoline industry has not been investigated in the otherwise very comprehensive reports by the Federal German Cartel Office. Due to the structure of the upstream level of the German gasoline market, there is a highly interdependent oligopoly or a joint natural monopoly since the vertically integrated gasoline enterprises jointly run refineries. Therefore, a natural monopoly that refines crude oil into gasoline is held by a group of enterprises. The definition of a natural monopoly does not include a 'joint natural monopoly'.

Independent of the exact legal definition, there needs to be close monitoring of highly concentrated industries. The German gasoline sector is an example of the possibilities of collusion that come along with highly concentrated industries.

4.9.3 Legal and Constitutional Restraints

An exchange or provision of information might interfere with an enterprise's protection of business secrets. Business secrets are also protected by fundamental rights of the GG, especially in Art. 2 GG, Art. 12 GG and Art. 14 GG. Consequently, the data processing procedures would have to adhere to strict data protection standards. In order for the measure to be proportional, there also have to be major reservations with regards to price discrimination. Additionally, milder tools with a similar effect to forwarding the price rationale to regulatory authorities should not exist.

4.9.4 Suggested Amendment

In order to prevent collusion at the upstream level, the Federal German Cartel Office should consider the efficiency of the upstream level of the market in the course of its comprehensive investigation. One way to conduct this assessment is by comparing the differences in raw material and wholesale prices of a particular market, product or service to other Western European countries.

This way it would be possible to determine whether or not vertically integrated enterprises engage in pricing activities that are intended to harm or in actual fact harm vertically non-integrated enterprises.

4.10 A Regulatory Regime Is Required that Focusses on the Challenges of Digital Networks (like Facebook) or Highly Integrated Market Place Enterprises (Such as Amazon)

4.10.1 Current Legal Obligation

The existing body of regulatory norms for digital markets is very small. Technically all regulatory acts are also applicable in the digital sphere, although some definitions as well as technology might not sufficiently capture the needs of digital markets.

4.10.2 Legal Shortcoming

Digital markets do not fit the traditional idea of market power according to economic theory. Enterprises like Amazon, Apple, Google, Microsoft or Facebook will argue that competition is "just one click away".

Still behavioural patterns in the digital sphere show the strong path dependencies. People do not use another search engine. Customers theoretically speaking have nearly unlimited options to choose another enterprise, but they do not purchase items elsewhere, interact on another platform or choose another platform to purchase items.

As a result of these developments, the economic theory on contestable markets does not sufficiently cover this phenomenon. The core factor in the theory of contestable markets needs to be the question of whether costumers are willing to switch the platform, the search engine or the enterprise.

4.10.3 Legal and Constitutional Restraints

When developing a regulatory regime for the digital sphere, the comprehensive set of fundamental rights and freedoms as outlined in Sect. 2.1.4 is applicable. Due to the comprehensiveness of the required legal amendments all of these norms need to be considered.

4.10.4 Suggested Legal Amendment

The crucial factor is having access to internet platforms. Additional regulation might even be needed for profit margins which is the case with energy or water distribution enterprises. Generally speaking, the regulatory regimes need to tailor-make their definitions for digital markets.

Chapter 5
Conclusion

The initial question of this investigation was to determine the effect of vertical integration on competitiveness of markets and to develop measures that would either stimulate competition through amendments of the system or reintroduce competition by means of unbundling.

In conclusion, there is a significant need for the improvement and protection of competition in markets. The German competition regime is well developed and very sophisticated, but there are still various necessities for legal amendments. Based on the model to assess the impact of vertical integration, there are sectors that would require a stricter regulatory regime in order to increase and stimulate competition.

There is a whole set of legal amendments that is expected to foster competition and lead to lower consumer prices. These measures range from simply continuing the work of competition and regulation authorities as well as educating consumers on the functioning of markets. This measure in particular is a response to counter the pitfalls and shortcomings of transparency. On the one hand, transparency can enable consumers to make a better choice. On the other hand, it may facilitate collusion among vertically integrated enterprises and provide them with comprehensive monitoring mechanisms. In this regard, transparency is a double-edged sword. In order to successfully regulate enterprises, regulation authorities need more data. Comprehensive price information as well as other information gives enterprises an advantage compared to regulation authorities.

Furthermore, there are means like the refusal to supply or capacity shortages that have not been dealt with sufficiently in the legal codes for regulation in Germany. Some vertically integrated enterprises in highly concentrated markets possess characteristics that may have a negative effect on the competitiveness of single markets.

Nevertheless, it is not necessary to unbundle or separate vertically integrated enterprises, unless it is a last resort.

C. Kleineberg, *Vertical Integration and Regulation*, SpringerBriefs in Law,
https://doi.org/10.1007/978-3-030-11358-2_5

The suggested amendments of competition law codes and measures in the German Act against Restraints of Competition can be primarily but not necessarily exclusively implemented to increase the competitiveness of markets.

Additionally, the digital sphere has yet to experience regulation that is tailor-made for its characteristics. In the case of digital markets, several definitions are not applicable and therefore need to be adjusted to the market's needs.

A field for further research could be to quantify the effect that a legal amendment in individual sectors has on competitiveness and societal welfare. A comparative approach with possible differences in methodology would allow for the effect of regulatory means to be quantified.

In the end, regulatory means, their implementation and monitoring costs could be weighed against their welfare effects and as well as their effect on competition.

MIX
Papier aus verantwortungsvollen Quellen
Paper from responsible sources
FSC® C105338

If you have any concerns about our products,
you can contact us on
ProductSafety@springernature.com

In case Publisher is established outside the EU,
the EU authorized representative is:
Springer Nature Customer Service Center GmbH
Europaplatz 3, 69115 Heidelberg, Germany

Printed by Libri Plureos GmbH
in Hamburg, Germany